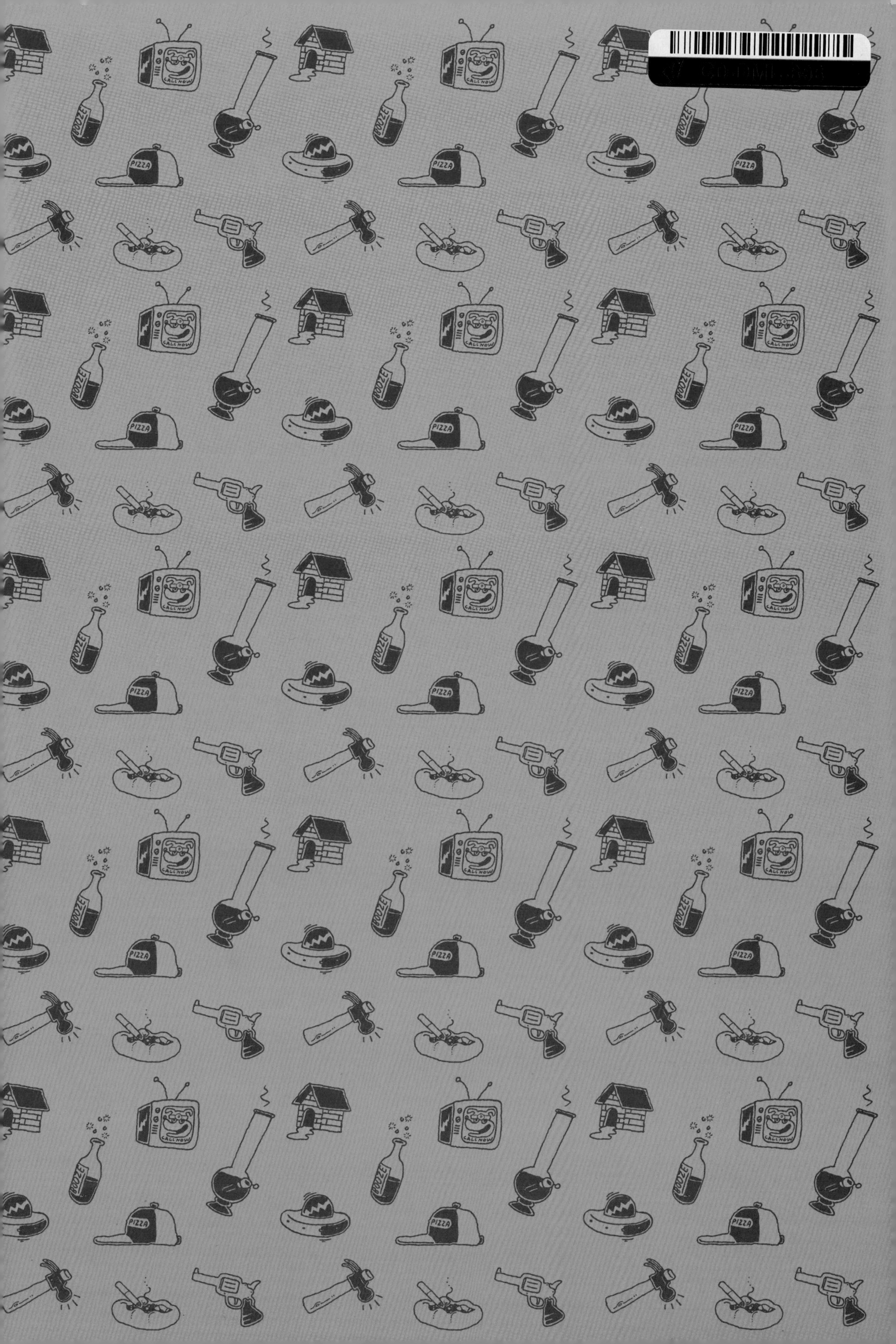
BOOZE!
PIZZA
CALL NOW

ROADS Publishing
19-22 Dame Street
Dublin 2
Ireland

www.roads.co

First published 2015
1
Funny-Hahas

Design and layout copyright
© ROADS Publishing
Image and text copyright
© Ted Gudlat
Design by Rinky / rinkydesign.com

Printed in Turkey

All rights reserved. No part of this production may be reprinted or reproduced or utilised in any form, or by any electronic, mechanical or other means, now known or hereafter invented, including photocopying and recording, or in any information storage or retrieval system, without the written consent of the Publisher.

This book is sold subject to the condition that it shall not, by way of trade or otherwise, be circulated in any form of binding or cover other than that in which it is published.

978-1-909399-41-9

FUNNY-HAHAS

TED GUDLAT

ROADS
PUBLISHING

"ONE DAY AT A TIME SLURPIE... JUST TAKE IT ONE DAY AT A TIME."

PIZZA SAUCE →

FAST CAR INSURANCE
FUTURE POWER
TOYS
INFOCORP
INFO2 CORP
CARS
DRINK
CARTOONS
PETS
NEWS
INTERNET
INVESTMENTS CO.
BANK
DRINKS
HOTEL
BREAD
DIAMONDS
MALL
GUNS
SEX:
STOP
MONOPOLY
SHIT
STADIUM
FREE: HAIR
BAR.
BEERSTORE
CIGARETTES
SCHOOL
SALE
BEER
PIZZA
SHOESTORE

THE INTRO:
CLICK.
CH
VOL.
AT SLURPIE'S TREE FORT HOME:
HAHA
ARE YOU...
...TIRED OF COMPLICATIONS?
BON VOYAGE
YOUR OWN YACHT!
LIFE COULD BE EASY!
1-800-DOG-EAT-DOGS
HA HA.
CALL IMMEDIATELY!
TAKE CONTROL!
VROOM VROOM
YOU'RE WORTH IT!!
TEST YOUR LIMITS
POKE
YUCK, YUCK!
MOON
EARTH
FORM MUSCLES!
GET SMART...
IT DOESN'T EVEN HURT!
WOW
FAST!!!!
FOOD WILL TASTE BETTER.
DELICIOUS!
TAP
CH.
VOL.
IMPRESS OTHER SPECIES!
WOOF!
MEOW!
CH.
VOL.
GROW...
HAIR!
COOL
CALL NOW!
WOW!
AND OUR STORY BEGINS...

BRIDGE LIFE!
YOU FIND ANYTHING IN THERE?
NOPE, NOTHIN! HOW ABOUT YOU?
-YICK.
OH YEAH, THERE'S SOMETHING IN HERE!
NOT SURE WHAT THE HECK IT IS THOUGH.
LEMME SEE! I KNOW A THING OR TWO ABOUT TRASH CANS.
HMMMMM... STRANGE.
YEAH! SURE IS...

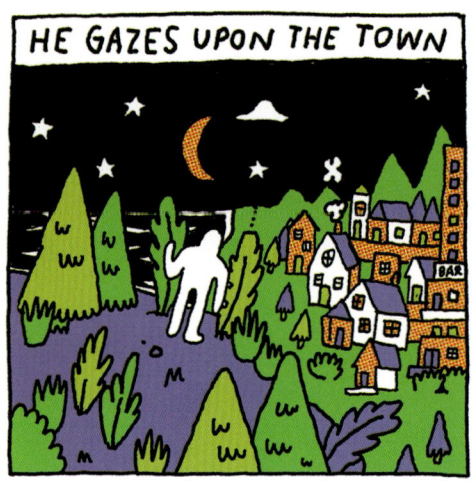

Wanderin'

DAY TURNS TO NIGHT.

MAYBE THIS PLACE IS FOR ME?

HE GAZES UPON THE TOWN

YOINK

MUNCH MUNCH MUNCH

ZIP

INTERESTING

HMMM.

I WONDER WHAT THIS SIGN SAYS... TOO BAD I CAN'T READ.

BAR

OPEN

AHHH-HHHHH HHH!

POOR GUY.

MEANWHILE:
24 HOUR-CONVENIE
OPEN
GIVE US ALL THE FUCKIN' MONEY!
!
YEAH GIVE US ALL THE MONEY, DIPSHIT!
I'M NEW, I DON'T KNOW HOW TO OPEN THE REGISTER WITHOUT MAKING A SALE!
PLEASE DON'T SHOOT ME.
UH-OH
W.T.F. IS THIS GUY DOING?
I DUNNO.
ALRIGHT BLAST THIS FOOL.
KLICK CLICK
SCRATCH
UH HUH!
R.I.P. KERRY
SPLAT!
NOT 2 ... MINORS
BUY CIGARETTES
DING!
$ $ $ $ $

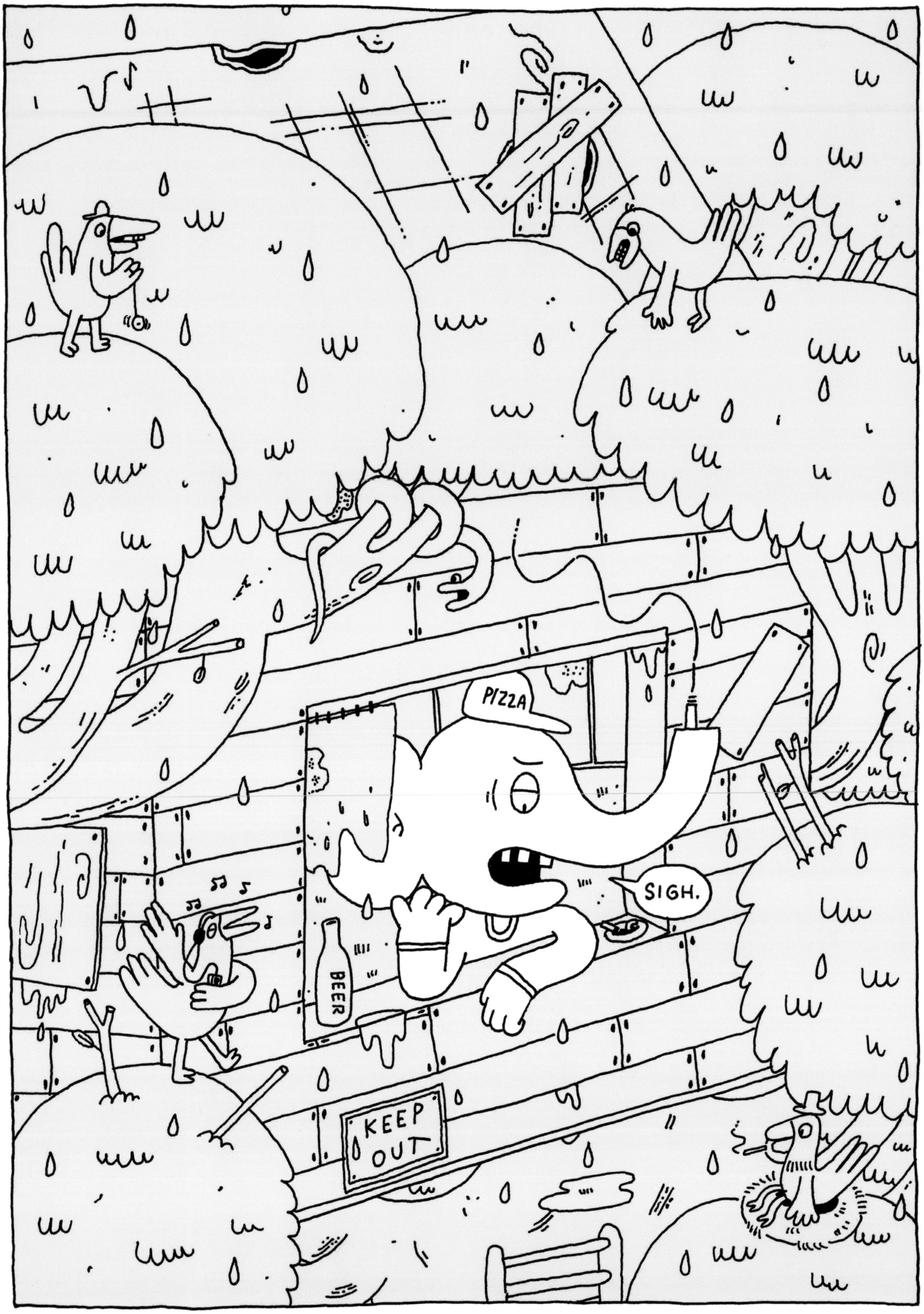
PIZZA
SIGH.
BEER
KEEP OUT

I'M SO HUNGOVER! I FEEL LIKE THE GARBAGE MAN.
ME TOO!
I WONDER WHAT HAPPENED TO MARV?
HMM!
WHERE AM I? WHAT TIME IS IT? I'M GONNA SLEEP IN THIS STUPID BOAT. HAHA.
PERFECT!
Z Z Z Z Z Z Z Z
HA HA HA HA HA HA HA HA HA
HA HA!
HA HA HA HA HA
BURP!
HA HA HA HA HA HA HA HA!
STRANDED.

DAYTIME TELEVISION
11:05AM
267 HURON DR.
BLAH
BLAH
BLAH
BLAH
BLAB LAB BLAH BLAH BLAH BLUH
BUB LAH BLH BLAH BLA
BUB LAH BLAH.
BLAH BLAH BLAH BLUH BABLAH?
BUZZZZZZZT...
BUZZZT.
BLAH BLAH BLAH BLAH
BLAH BLAH
BLAH BLAH!
SIGH.
END.

TELEVISION SPECIAL:
THE DOLPHIN KEY
PART ONE
HMMM.
HMMM.
HMMM.
I THINK I KNOW JUST THE THING.
T.B.C.

BONUS! FLAVOUR COUNTRY.
DECENT
CIGAR-ETTES
WHAT THE FUCK IS THIS ANCIENT BULL SHIT!
DVD BOX SET
NOT BAD.
THERE HAS GOT TO BE SOMETHING WORTH MY WHILE IN THIS SHIT POND!
DISGUSTING!
GARBAGE.
GROSS.
ARF!
IT'S BIG!
TUG.
HELP!

"THE COMIC ABOUT THE CATS IN THE NEIGHBOURHOOD 1."
MEOW MUH MEOW
ROOOW!
MEOW ROWW MEOW
MEOWIE?
MEOW MUH!
MOOOW!
MEOW
MEOW REOW
MEOW MOW YOW?
MEOW
MUH...
POKE.
STAB!
TWIST
GUSH!
MEOW MEOWW.
MEOW?

HEY MISTER, HEY MISTER! JUST TO LET YOU KNOW YOUR CAT FOUGHT A DOG AND THE DOG GOT HURT.
SIGH
OH YEAH AND YOUR CAT BIT THE NEIGHBOUR AND THEY JUST WANT TO KNOW IF HE HAS GOT HIS SHOTS.
OOH, AND MY CAT HAD A KITTEN, SO IF YOU SEE IT LET ME KNOW! IT'S TOO FAST FOR ME TO CATCH.
OHH, AND MY DAD BROKE A HOLE IN THE WINDOW OF YOUR DOOR PLAYING HOCKEY WITH A ROCK! HE'S SORRY.
OHH, AND THE LANDLORD WAS KNOCKING ON YOUR DOOR ALL DAY TODAY, HE WANTS YOU TO PAY RENT.
MISTER!? MISTER!
COOL.

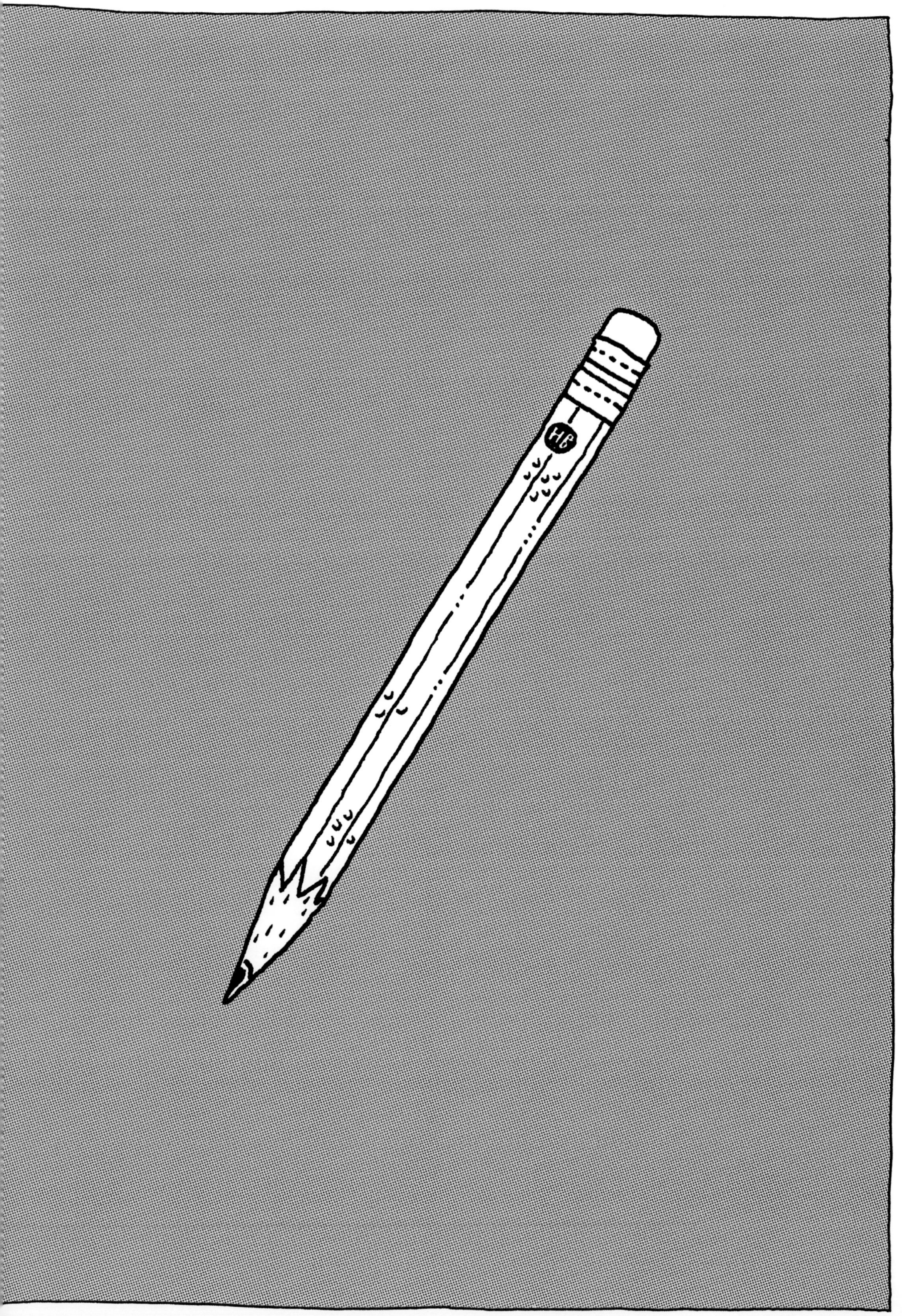
HB

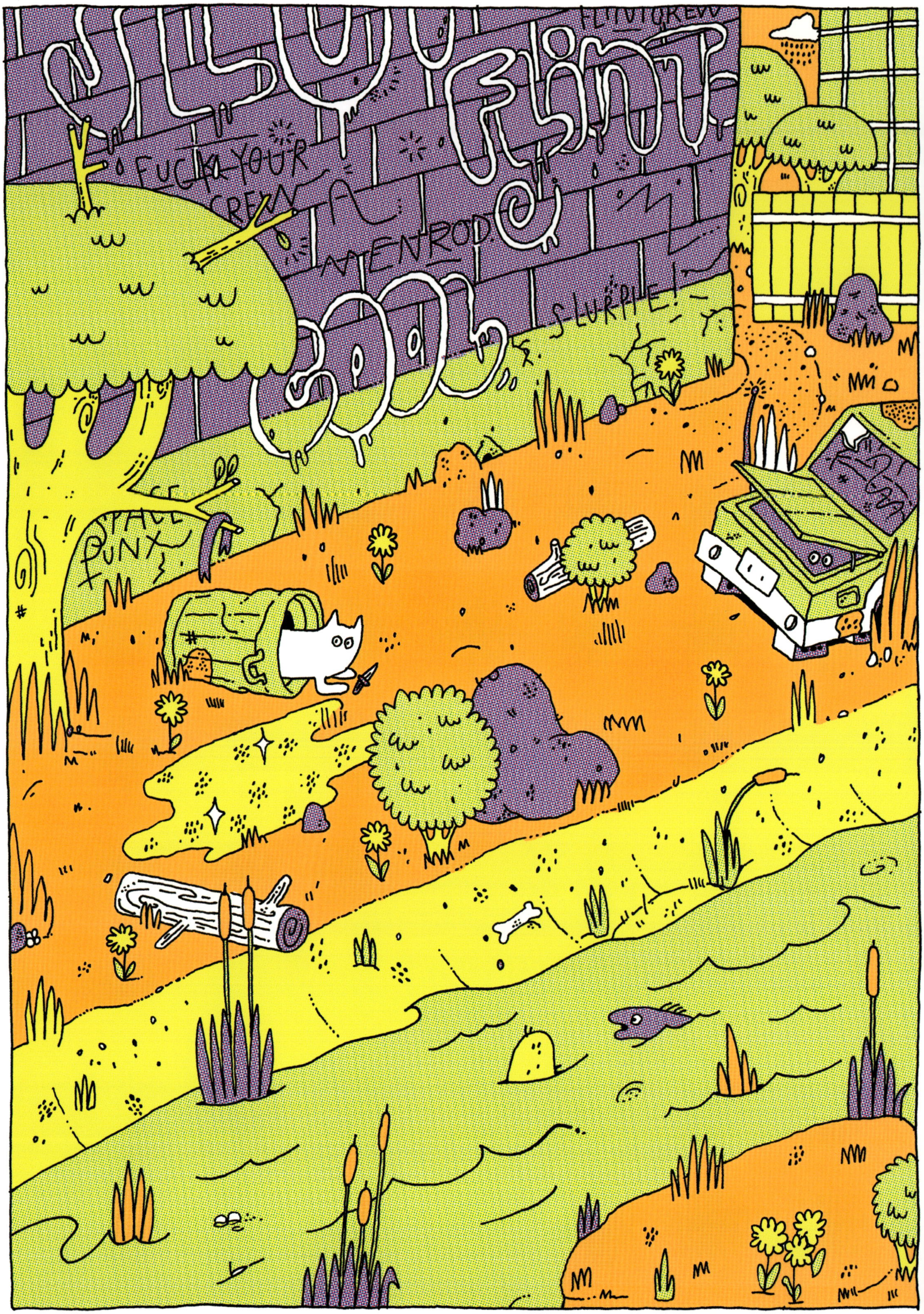
FUCK YOUR CREW
SLURPIE!

CONTENTS OF SLURPIE'S SEDAN.
BOOZE
WINE
STRONG BEER
CANAD-IAN RYE WHISKEY
BEER
A JAR
TIPS
FULL OF MONEY COINS.
HAND GUN
'CAUSE YOU NEVER KNOW
KETCHUP CHIPS
KETCHUP POTATO CHIPS
NO TRANS FATS?
OF COURSE
A GIANT GARBAGE BAG
OF EMPTIES.
WEIRD FUCKED UP
FUNNYHAHAS
COMIC BOOKS
A FILTHY
WATER PIPE
A PIZZA
PIECE OF PIZZA
HE FORGOT TO DELIVER
BEAR TRAP
FOR COMIC RELIEF
PORTABLE CD PLAYER
CD ANTI-SHOCK
WITH BURNT CDS
½ OUNCE
SLURPIE'S
O.G. KUSH
WELL FOLKS THAT'S MY CAR!
PIZZA

LANDLORD SITUATION

Knock knock knock

"Have you paid rent yet?"
"Nope."

"Oh shit it's him. Pretend we're not home."
"Duck!"

Knock knock knock!

"I've been doing this all week."
"Why don't you just tell him we have no money?"

"I could..."

"But he's EVIL!"

NO FUNDS

BAND PRACTICE
ONE
TWO
THREE
FOUR!
AT SLURPIE'S HOUSE:
TTT
TTT
TTT
SMACK
TTT
TTT
TTT
TTTTT TTTTT
WHY DO I HANG OUT WITH SUCH LOSERS?
OOWWWWWW!
OWWWW
...WWWW
DING
DING
DING
DING
...WWWW!
DING DING
DING
DING
DING
DING
DING
SMASH
SMASH.
OWWWWWWW!
SMASH!
SMASH
DING.
OWWW.
UGH.
WE FUCKIN' RULE!
SMASH.

HAUNTED HOUSE: 422 ROSE DR.
DOES SOMEONE LIVE HERE?
NOBODY HAS LIVED HERE FOR YEARS!
THIS PLACE IS SO CREEPY.
I KNOW! IT'S DILAPIDATED.
TAP TAP.
LOOK AT THIS FUCKED UP ART!
GIVES ME THE CREEPS.
THEY MUST HAVE BEEN PART OF A CULT OR SOMETHING!
FUCKED!
THERE IS STILL FOOD IN THIS FRIDGE!
I HATE THIS PLACE! LET'S LEAVE.
NOT YET!
PRETTY NICE FOR AN ABANDONED SHIT HOLE.
NO! LET'S LEAVE NOW!
OH GOD! THERE'S LIGHT COMING FROM THIS ROOM!
SHHH-HHH.
GET OUT OF OUR HOUSE! YOU FOOLS!
OUT! OUT!
UGGGG!
UHHHHH-OHHH!
RUN!

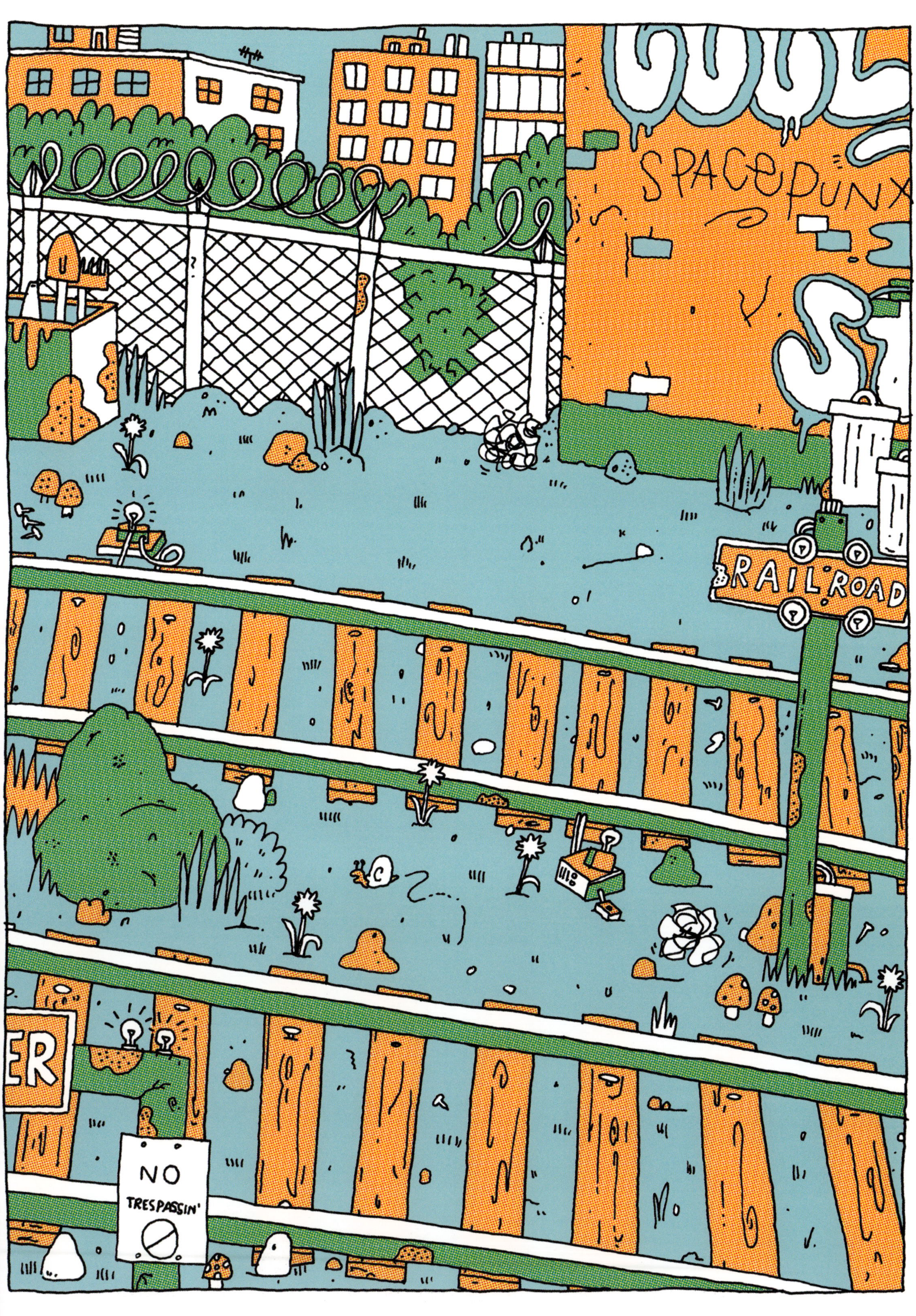
SPACEPUNX
RAILROAD
NO TRESPASSIN'
ER

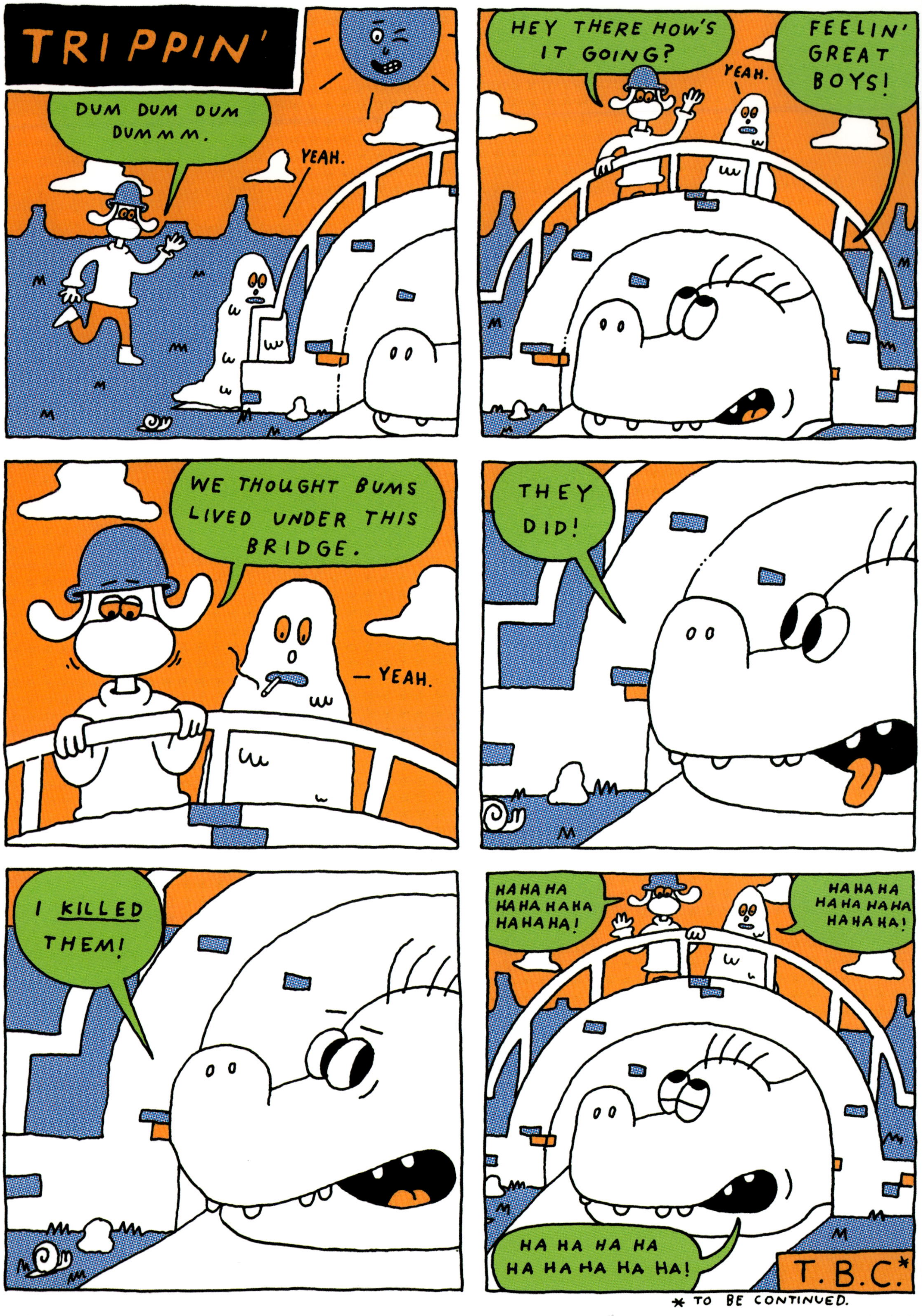

* TO BE CONTINUED.

SLEEPIN' IN FEELS REAL GOOD!
HOLY FUCK! WHAT A LONG NIGHT. I HATE DELIVERING PIZZAS.
SLAM!
2 A.M. ALREADY!
SLEEP AT LAST.
YAWN
MONDAY
RING
RING
TUESDAY
RING
RI
WEDNESDAY
RING
RING
RING
THURSDAY
RING
RING
RING
FRIDAY
RING
RING
RING
RING
RING
RING
UH, AH, SLURPIE HERE, TALK TO ME!
SLURPIE I'M JUST CALLING TO TELL YOU THAT YOU'RE FIRED!
FUCK!
DING

PUSH
ON
CH
VOL
HANGING AT E-DOGS HOUSE!
HEY YOU!
ARE MENIAL TASKS GIVING YOU GRIEF?
OUCH.
SSSSSSSSTTT.
CH.
VOL.
YOU COULD SPEND
CHA CHING
TRILLIONS!
BUT IF YOU CALL IN THE NEXT 12 MINUTES!
BANG
GIFT
12
MINS.
YOU'LL GET A FREE GIFT!
BUT REMEMBER CALL IN THE NEXT 12 MINUTES..
HAHA.
FREE FISH WITH EVERY GUN!
AND WE'LL THROW IN A SECOND GIFT ABSOLUTELY FREE!
HA HA HA HA HA HA HA
YOU
LIMO
DRIVER
DON'T WASTE YOUR TIME!!! LIVE THE LIFE YOU WANT TO LIVE!!!
CALL! CALL! CALL! CALL! CALL! CALL! CALL! CALL! CALL!
CH
VOL
CALL NOW AND WE WILL SEND YOU 3 WHOLE VIDEO TAPES FULL OF MORE GREAT OFFERS!
DEALS
VOL. I
BUY
VOL. II
WOW
VOL. III
"WE CALL IT THE ULTIMATE OFFER BUYERS PACKAGE!!!
DON'T LET OTHERS BEAT YOU TO IT.
FINISH-LINE
NOW A MESSAGE FROM THE COUNTY POLICE DEPARTMENT.
HA
...
HAVE YOU SEEN HIM?
POLICE
MISSING PERSON: KERRY Z.
CH
VOL

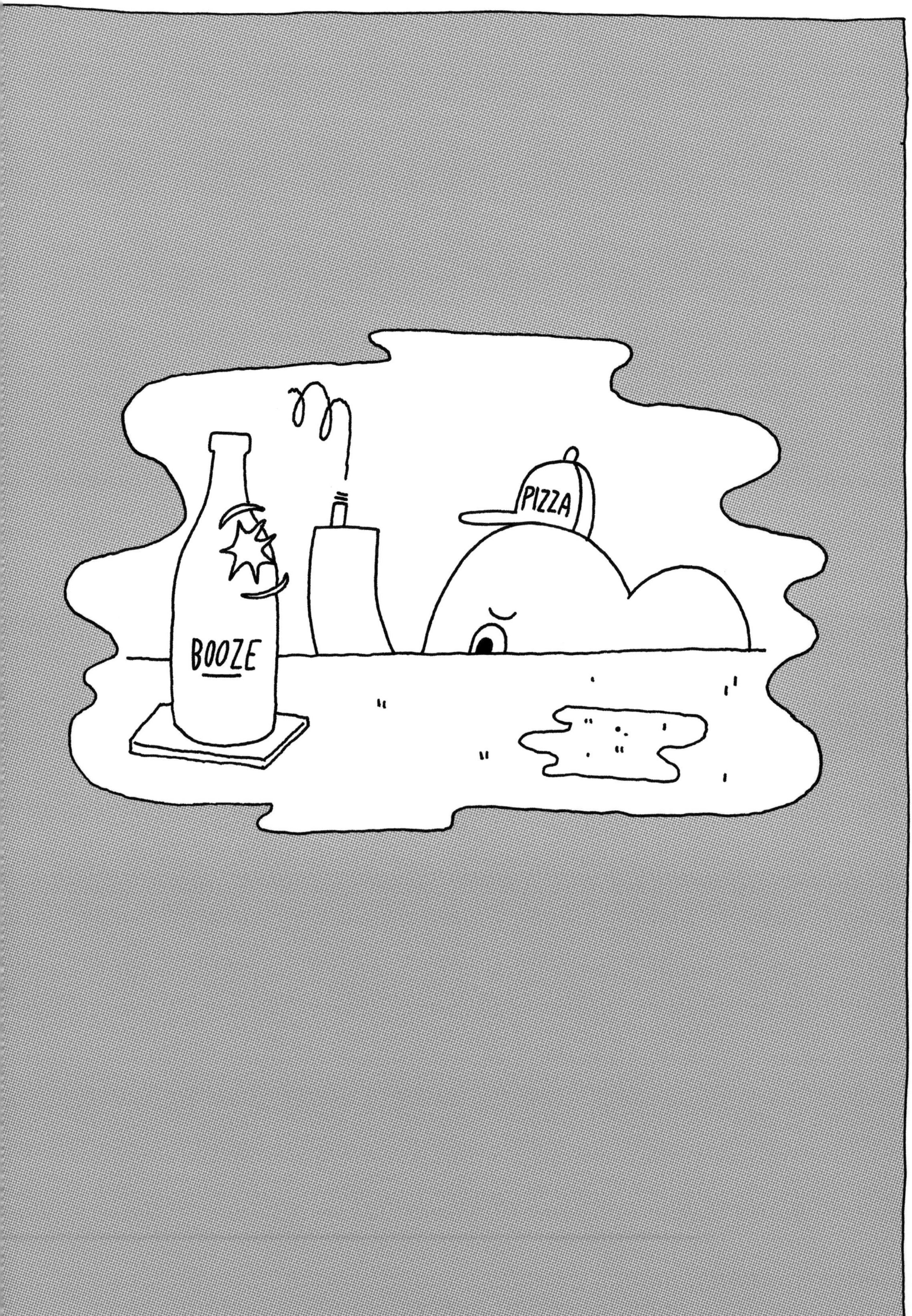
BOOZE
PIZZA

NIGHT AT NICK'S
HEY WHERE ARE YOU HEADED!
I'M GOING TO NICK'S PIZZA BAR.
AWESOME! IT'S LIKE DRINKING IN A MALL.
YAH! BEER'S ONLY 10$ A PITCHER!
COOL! CAN I COME.
YEAH SURE.
PIZZA
HEY YOU IDIOTS. WHERE YOU GOING?
NICK'S PIZZA BAR. THE FRIENDLIEST PLACE IN TOWN.
LET'S DO THIS SHIT.
OKAY!
LOOK AT THIS LOOSE ASS CREW YOU'VE ASSEMBLED. WHERE'S THE PARTY BABIES?
HAHA NICK'S PIZZA BAR. IT'S KARAOKE NIGHT. LET'S GO.
PIZZA
NICK'S PIZZA BAR
BEER
LOOK THERE IT IS!
YES!
BANKRUPT. CLOSED FOREVER.
WHAT? NO WAY.

THE DOLPHIN KEY PT. 2

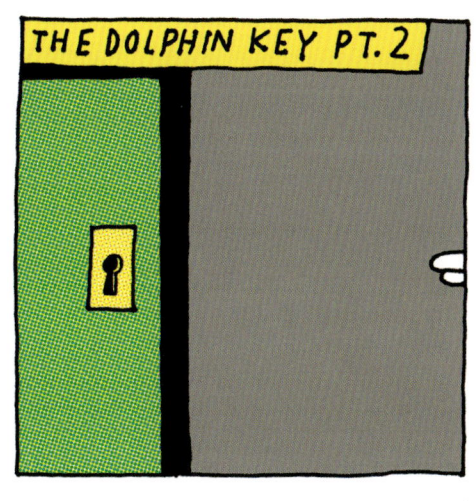

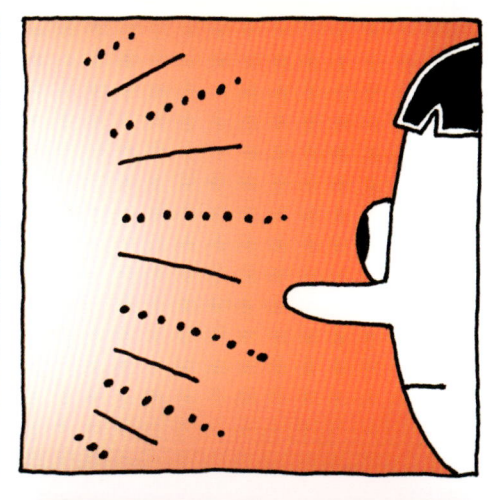

CLICK

TWIST

I GUESS THE DOLPHIN WAS THE KEY.

HOME SWEET HOME
NOT AGAIN.
GROAN!
OHHH NO!
?
SIGH
PICKLES
WHY DO I DO THIS TO MYSELF?
FUCK!
SWOOSH...
SMACK...
DONK!
SPACE-PUNX
LIVE AT THE SALOON SPACE PUNKS
SLURPIE
GROAN

FRIENDS 4 EVER
I HIT MYSELF LAST NIGHT, I THINK I HAVE A CONCUSSION.
OH.
YEAH.
IS THAT BECAUSE YOU HATE YOURSELF AND WANT TO DIE?
YEAH.
YEAH I'VE DONE THAT.
HMMM.
...USUALLY WHEN I HIT MYSELF I DON'T WANT TO DIE.
?
SIP.
IT'S BECAUSE I JUST WANT TO FALL ASLEEP.
YEAH!
FOREVER.
YEAH.
YEAH.
SAD.

BUSINESS AS USUAL
INFOCORP
INFO2 CORP
WE BROUGHT THE PROTOTYPE.
WHERE IS THE MONEY?
RUB RUB
HERE'S THE MONEY! NOW WHERE'S THE PROTOTYPE?
POP
$1000
ALRIGHT... RELEASE IT!
YEAH.
BEEP
WAAHHG
"PROTOTYPE"
HA, HA, HA, MUAH, HA, HA, HA, HA!
EEWAHP GGUUO
LET'S GET OUT OF HERE.
YEAH THIS GUY IS NUTS.
GET THE MONEY.
ZOOM!
INFOCORP

BATHTUB.COMIC/TG14

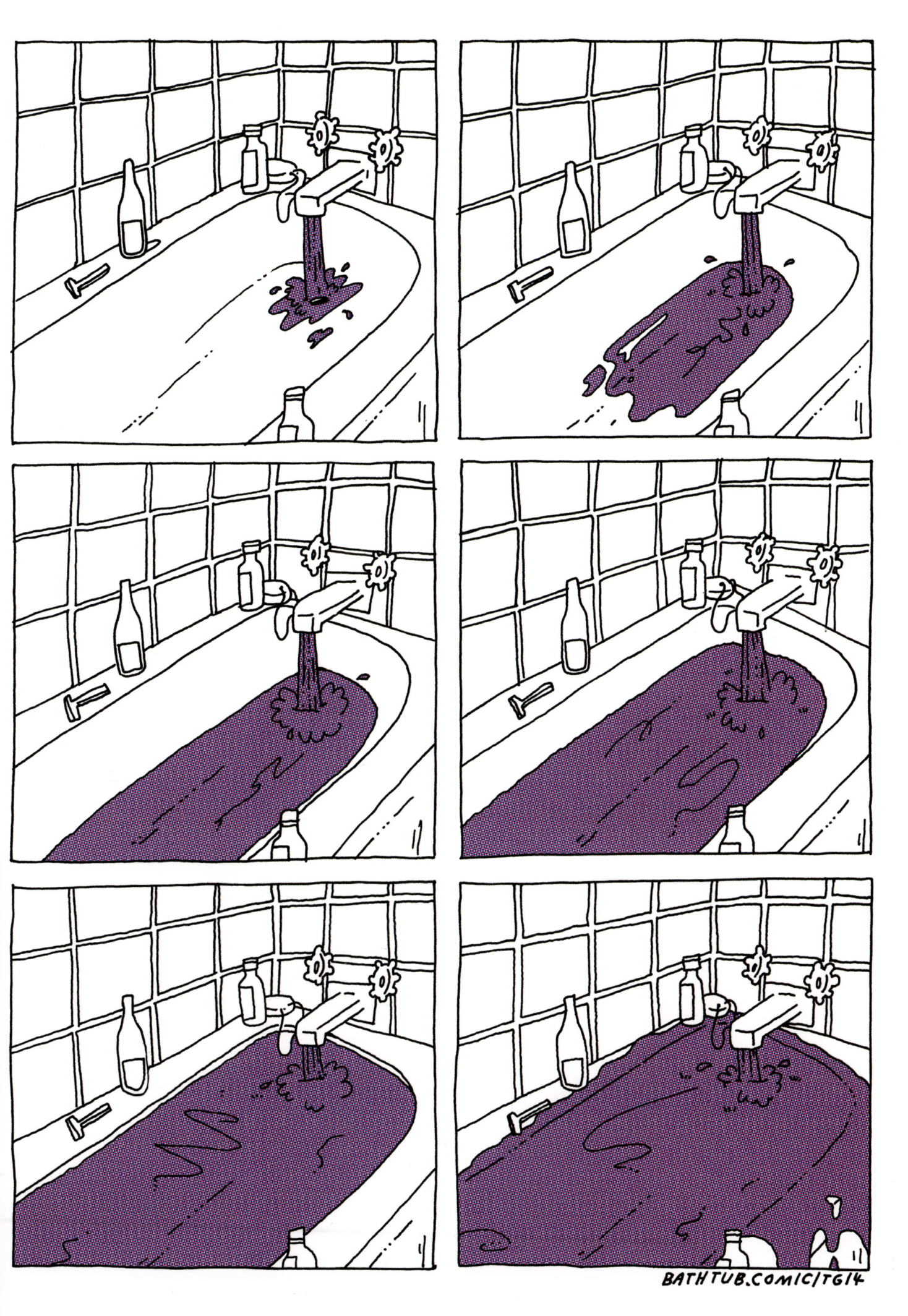

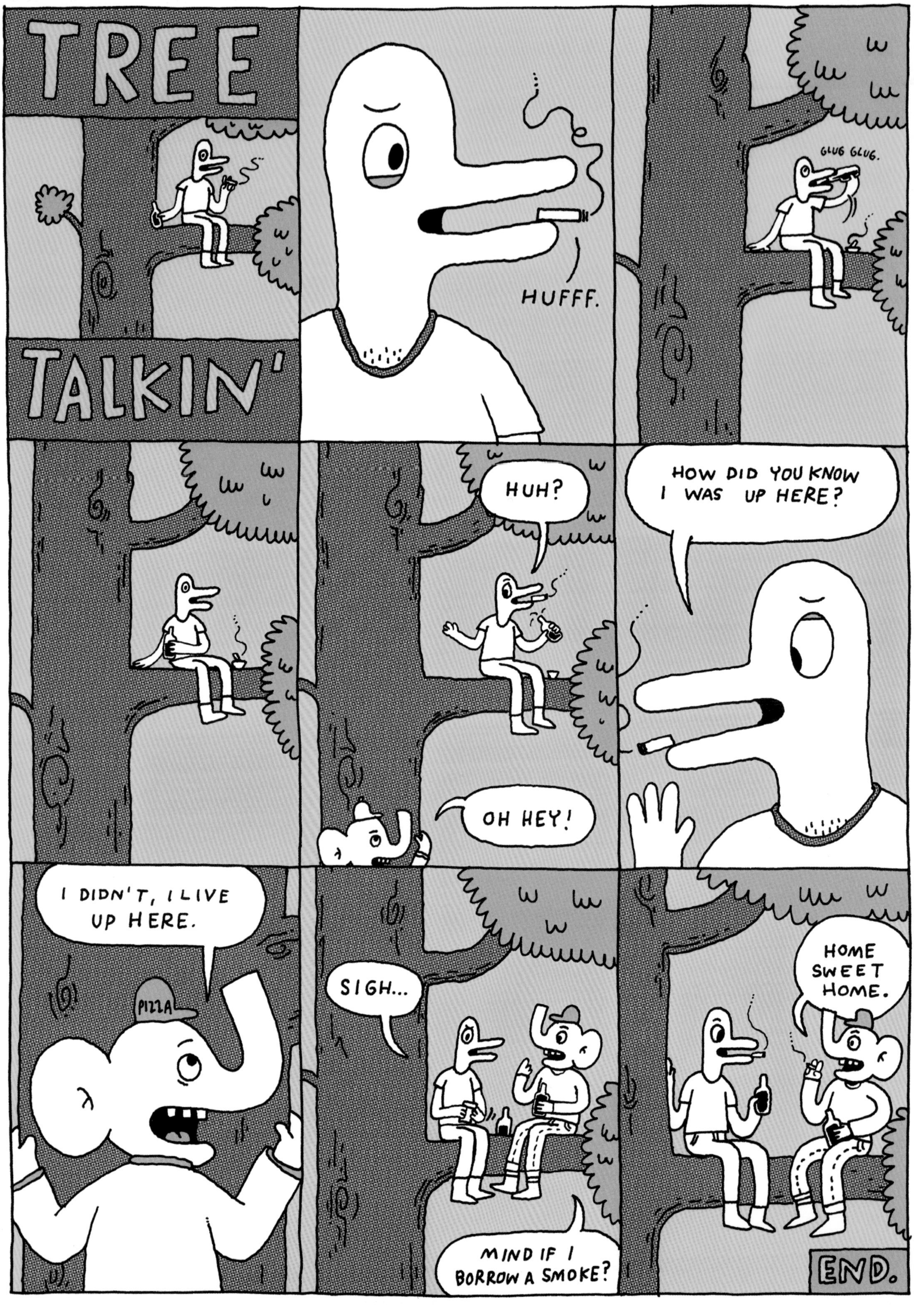
TREE
TALKIN'
HUFFF.
GLUG GLUG.
HUH?
OH HEY!
HOW DID YOU KNOW I WAS UP HERE?
I DIDN'T, I LIVE UP HERE.
PIZZA
SIGH...
MIND IF I BORROW A SMOKE?
HOME SWEET HOME.
END.

"THE COMIC ABOUT THE CATS IN THE NEIGHBOURHOOD 2."
MEOW.
MEOW ME?
BROOOOW!
CATNIP
MROOOWH!
MROEW!
MROW!
TAT TAT
TAT TAT
MEUH?
...
TAT
TAT
TAT
TAT
TAT
TAT
TAT
TAT
TAT
TAT
TAT
TAT
MEOWW.

A SHORT BREAK: FOR THE DOGS' SAKE.
BLAH
FFP.
SHP SHP!
SLURP
SLURP
SLURP
ARF
POOT!
ZZZ
DUH!

PILOTS
A FOUR PANEL JOINT!
FUCK!!! GOD DAMMIT!
WHAT'S WRONG?
KICK
PIZZA
WE CAN'T BE PILOTS!
WHY NOT?
BECAUSE WE'VE DONE ACID.
SHIT!
THAT'S ONE OF THE QUESTIONS THEY ASK YOU WHEN YOU ARE BECOMING ONE.
DAMMIT.
IT WAS OUR DREAM.
THIS SUCKS!
TELL ME ABOUT IT.
AW SHIT!

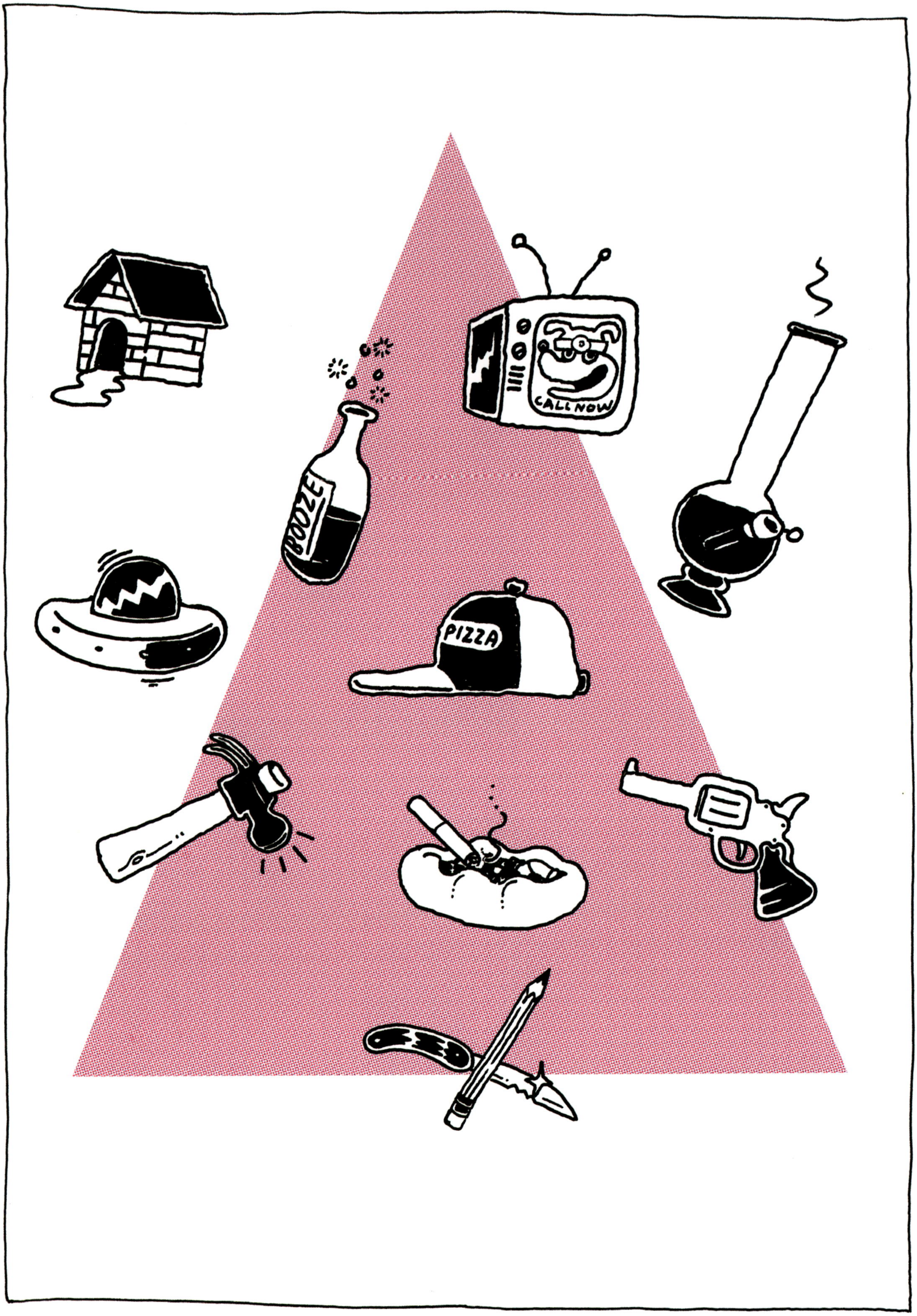
CALL NOW
BOOZE
PIZZA

WOW SOME COOL COLLECTABLE TRADING CARDS OF ALL YOUR FAVOURITE CHARACTERS FROM THIS VERY BOOK!
COLLECT ALL EIGHT!
VERY RARE.
BASEBALL DOG
I HATE THIS.
SMOOSHIE
TEA-CUP
YEE HAW!
CHIPSTER
MAD-DOG
CASPER
PHONE ME.
RANCE
LACIE
HMPH.
KYLE

TEACUP
POODLE-ISH

A serious critic of just about everything.

Smokes menthols.

Orders sparkling water.

Claims to be fluent in six different languages.

Drives a Civic.

SMOOSHIE
DARK SPIRIT

Summoned Christmas Eve 1999.

Knows how to seriously party.

Its hat has a higher I.Q. than it does.

Slowly deteriorating, I guess we all are.

NEW TECHNOLOGY

CHIPSTER
MULE

Came from the old country to find work.

Currently works on a nutmeg farm.

Can count up to 17.

Almost drowned once in 3 feet of water.

CASPER
SMART

Reads at a twelfth grade level.

Loves travelling even if it is just to get milk from the corner store.

B.E.D.M.A.S.

SOH, CAH, TOA.

"#1 SKIRMISHER"

MAD-DOG
JANITOR

91 years' old.

Cleans at a very efficient rate + works for very low wages.

Chews bubble gum.

Mop over sweep baby. Any day.

KYLE
CRINKLEY-DOG

Squeaks when he walks.

Squeaks when he talks.

Works for the govn't

Is going to court for tax fraud.

LACIE
GIRL

Loves all animals.

Shares a special bond with her pet "Bob"

Likes orange soda floats.

Fast.

RANCE
IDIOT

Beer, beer, beer, beer, beer, beer, beer.

Wine, wine, wine, wine, wine, wine, wine, wine.

Vomit.

Sleep, repeat.

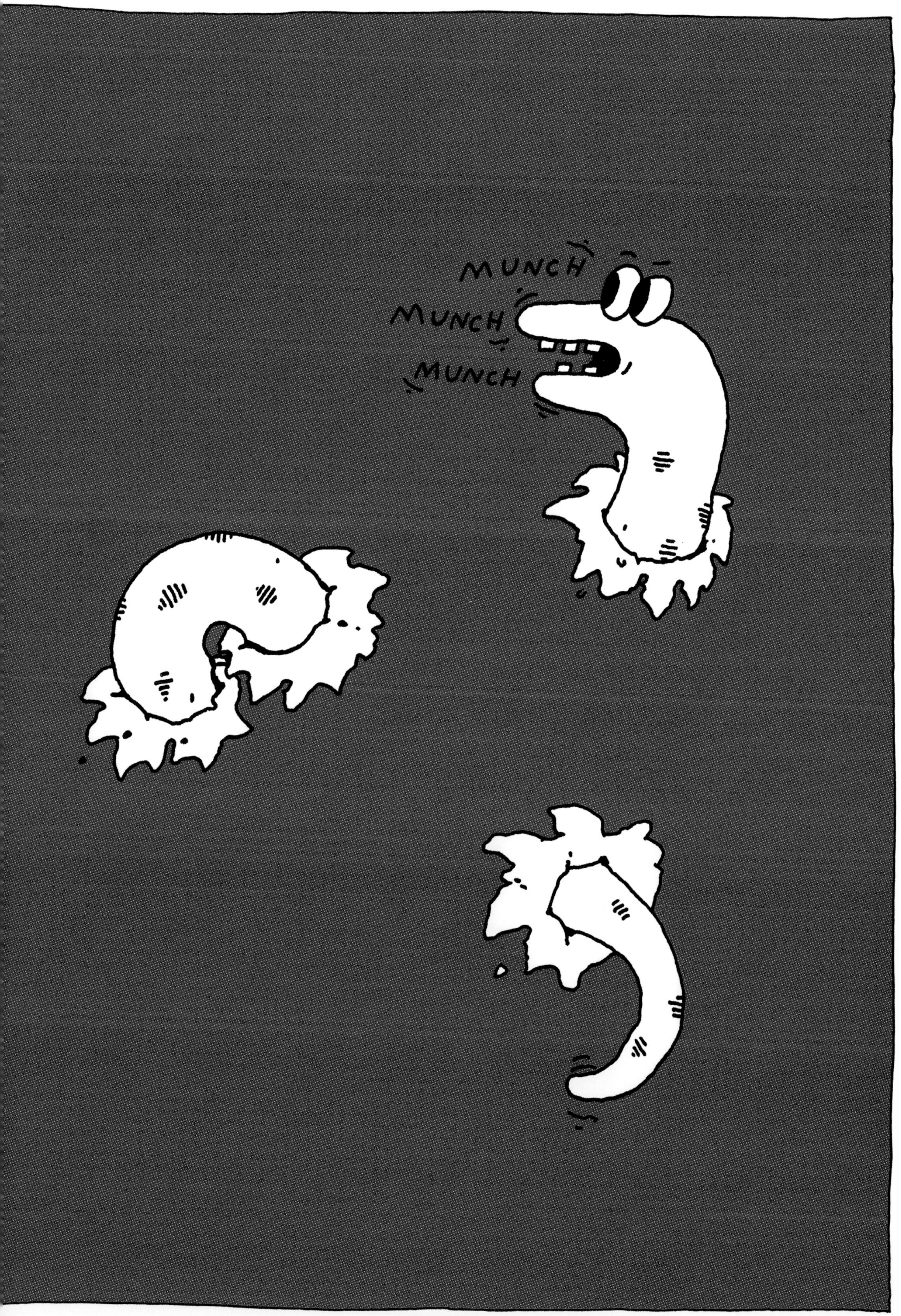
MUNCH
MUNCH
MUNCH

BAR NIGHT BRAWL
BAR
BIKER NITE!
HEY WAKE UP BACK THERE!
EERKKK
WE NEED BEERS!
A.S.A.P.
...?!
TWO BEERS FOR MY TWO FAVE BOYS.
HA HA.
GLUGG! LUGGG! GLUG! GLUG!
PIZZA
SMASH!
KA-BOMB.
WHOOSH.
BANG!
SMACK!
CRASH.
SMASH!
SLAP...
STAB!
AGGGG!
WACK.
THANK GOD WE GOT OUT OF THAT HELL HOLE!
EXIT
WHERE TO NEXT?
SUX!

CONTENTS OF SLURPIE'S STOMACH

"You've seen what's in my car. Now check out what's in my guts!"

	6 PACK	**PIZZA**
	"ALRIGHT" BEER	SOMEONE ELSE'S SLICE
1 WHOLE BOTTLE	**HOT DOGS**	**BOX OF WINE**
ROTI LADY HOT SAUCE	QUANTITY: 5	"CHEAP" (SHIT WINE / CABERNÉ BLANC CHAT)
NUCLEAR 'SHROOMS	**1 PACK OF GUM**	**1 BOTTLE**
3.5 GRAMS	NICOTINE GUM (QUIT TODAY GUM)	FLAVOUR-LESS MOUTH WASH (FANCY ORAL WASH)
B.B.Q.	**TOO MANY WEED COOKIES**	**CONDIMENTS**
PORK RIBS	LAMAR'S RECIPE: 2 oz.	LAST RESORT (KETCHUP, VINEGAR, MUSTARD, MAYO)

"ONE MORE DRINK FER THE ROAD DADDIO?"

HEY DALTON...
NOT RIGHT NOW LANCE. I'M OPERATING THIS SPACE CRAFT.
THIS IS KIND OF IMPORTANT.
I SAID I'M DRIVING!
BUT...
I'M IN LOVE WITH YOU!
WHAT! OUR SPECIES CAN NOT LOVE.
NOOO. I'M LIKE IN LOVE WITH YOU!
....
SILENCE.
AWKWARD.

WHEELIN AND DEALIN
7.0g.
ON
I'M REALLY HAPPY DEALER-JAY GOT BACK TO US. I AM JONEZIN'!
PIZZA
KNOCK
YEAH MAN, HE'S GOT GOOD SHIT. BUT HE'S AN IDIOT!
PIZZA
YAH!?
BOYS! ALWAYS A PLEASURE, COMM'ON IN!
UH, OK.
PIZZA
DOPE
YOU GUYS ARE IN LUCK TODAY. I'VE GOT SOME BOMB SHIT!
DOPE
MEOW LYFE
SNIFF
DOPE
PURP.
...BUT THIS IS THE CHRONIC SO IT COSTS MORE BUT IT'S WELL WORTH THE EXTRA DOUGH! TRUST.
YOU GUYS LOOKING FOR ANY OTHER PARTY FAVOURS? TONY? MOLLY? LIQUID G?
NAH JUST THE USUAL... THIRTY RIGHT?
PIZZA
DOPE
MEOW LYFE
HA HA THIRTY! TRY FORTY!
AW COMMON MAN WE'RE GOOD CUSTOMERS!
PIZZA
DOPE
MEOW LYFE
NOT REALLY.
SO WHAT, ARE YOU TWO GONNA STAY ALL NIGHT?
PIZZA
DOPE
MEOW LYFE
LET'S GO

INTERNET COMIC
PE
CLICK
CLICK
CLICK
EACE
SEEMS LEGIT.
INTERNET
CLICK! FOR COMPLETE HAPPINESS.
CLICK
CLICK
POOF!
BE CAREFUL THE INTERNET IS A TERRIBLE PLACE AND AROUND EVERY CORNER IS A TRICK!

PRETTY GIRLS
WARNING: EXPLICT CONTENT. MATURE READERS ONLY.
OMG! FUCK OFF!
TTYL.
FUCKING SHIT BRITT!
ROFL.
UHH HUHH! OMG I LOVE THAT EFFIN' SONG MAKES ME FEEL SOOO CHILL!
...I KNOW WTF!
YAAH! I LIKE GOT TO THE PARTY AND WAS LIKE "WHERE'S THE BLOW!"
LOLZ! HA HA I KNOW!
DON'T BE A FUCKING BITCH BRITTNEY!
YAAA BUT I'M JUST AN INTELLIGENT GIRL LOOKING FOR A SMART HOT GUY!
OMG! WHAT THE FUCK WAS SHE WEARING? I HOPE SHE DIES IN THE SAME GUTTER SHE FOUND THAT OUTFIT IN.
WHAT?
NOO! I'M A PARTY GIRL! LET'S GET FUCKED UP!
I NEED A CIGARETTE!! I'LL DIE IF I CAN'T HAVE ONE!
I'M GOING ON A DIET! I'M SO FUCKING FAT! COMMON' LOOK AT ME!
I'M SUCHA FUCKING LARD CAKE! I NEED TO LOSE AT LEAST 80 POUNDS!
DICTIONARY
DVD
BIBLE
FUNNY HAHAS
PHOTO ALBUM
BIG SHITS 2010
COMIXXX
SMUT
BRITTNEY? BRITTNEY?
WHAT THE FUCK JUST HAPPENED?

NUTMEGGER'S
SUPPORT YOUR LOCAL *COUGH* SCAM ARTIST?
NUTMEG
WHAT'D YOU SAY?
AHHH, NOTHING. WANNA BUY SOME NUTMEG?
SURE!! I LOVE THIS STUFF DEEELICIOUS!
THANKS!
IDIOT! THAT'S JUST GROUND UP WOOD. HAHA.
COMING SOON TO A THEATRE NEAR YOU.

OK LAMAR I'LL BE BACK SOON. JUST CHILL OUT AND DON'T FUCK ANYTHING UP WHILE I'M GONE.
PIZZA
YAA MAN, I'M THE KING OF CHILLING!
SPARK.
PUFFF.
PASS OUT!
ZZZ
DROP
= BAD
UH-OH
OH GOD
ZZZZ
POP
OH SHIT!
SMASH!
AHHH!
ROAR
GULP. AW SHIT. SLURPIE AIN'T GONNA LIKE THIS ONE BIT.
RUB
SAD DAY.

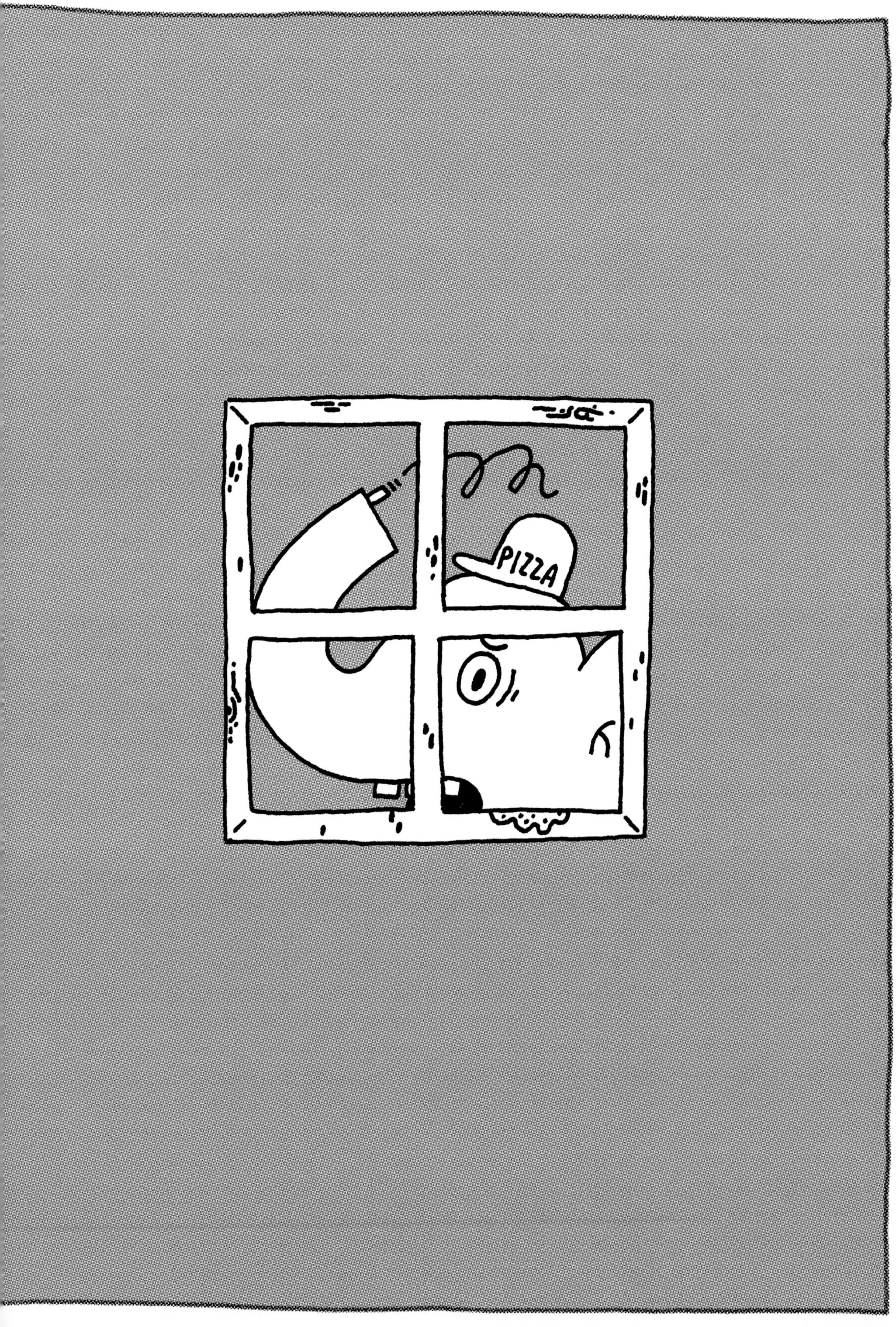
PIZZA

THE OL' MINE
MINE CLOSED
HANGING OUT AT THE OL' MINE:
SURE IS DARK IN HERE.
YA DUMBIE! IT'S AN ABANDONED MINE.
PIZZA
I'VE GOT AN IDEA. LET'S CRACK A BREW.
PIZZA
KASSSST.
CHEEEEERS.
CLINK.
THERE IS NOTHING LIKE GETTING WASTED INSIDE A MOUNTAIN.
PIZZA
AM I RIGHT?
AM I... WHA WHA WHOA!
POW
HEY CHECK OUT WHAT I FOUND DOWN HERE!
BURP!
IT'S AN OLD TIMEY SCROLL OR SOMETHING.
DON'T TRUST THE TELEVISION.
-OLD TIMES

"SCROOCHED IN"
WAIT SO YOU ARE TELLIN' ME YOU'VE NEVER BEEN SCROOCHED IN BEFORE!
NOPE, NEVER.
K
DING! DING! DING! DING! DING! DING! DING! DING!
"SCROOCH" BELL
WOOOHOOO! WE'RE GITTIN' SCROOCHED TONIGHT!
WOOOO!
UH-OH!
K
YEEEHAW! GITTIN' SCROOOOOOCH'D!
KISS THE FISH! KISS THE FISH!
SMOOCH THAT SLIPPERY FUCK'N FISH!
TAKE THE SHOT!
HA HA WOOHOO!
IN 4 LIFE

SLURPIE'S LAMENT

HERE LIE THE REMAINS OF SLURPIE'S HOME.

HMPH.

GLUG GLUG

DEVASTATING.

CLUTCH
TWIST

POW

STAY THE HELL AWAY FROM ME LAMAR! WE ARE NOT FRIENDS ... ... ANYMORE!

TOSS

YOU FUCKED UP TOO BAD THIS TIME.

I GUESS I DESERVE THIS

FINI.

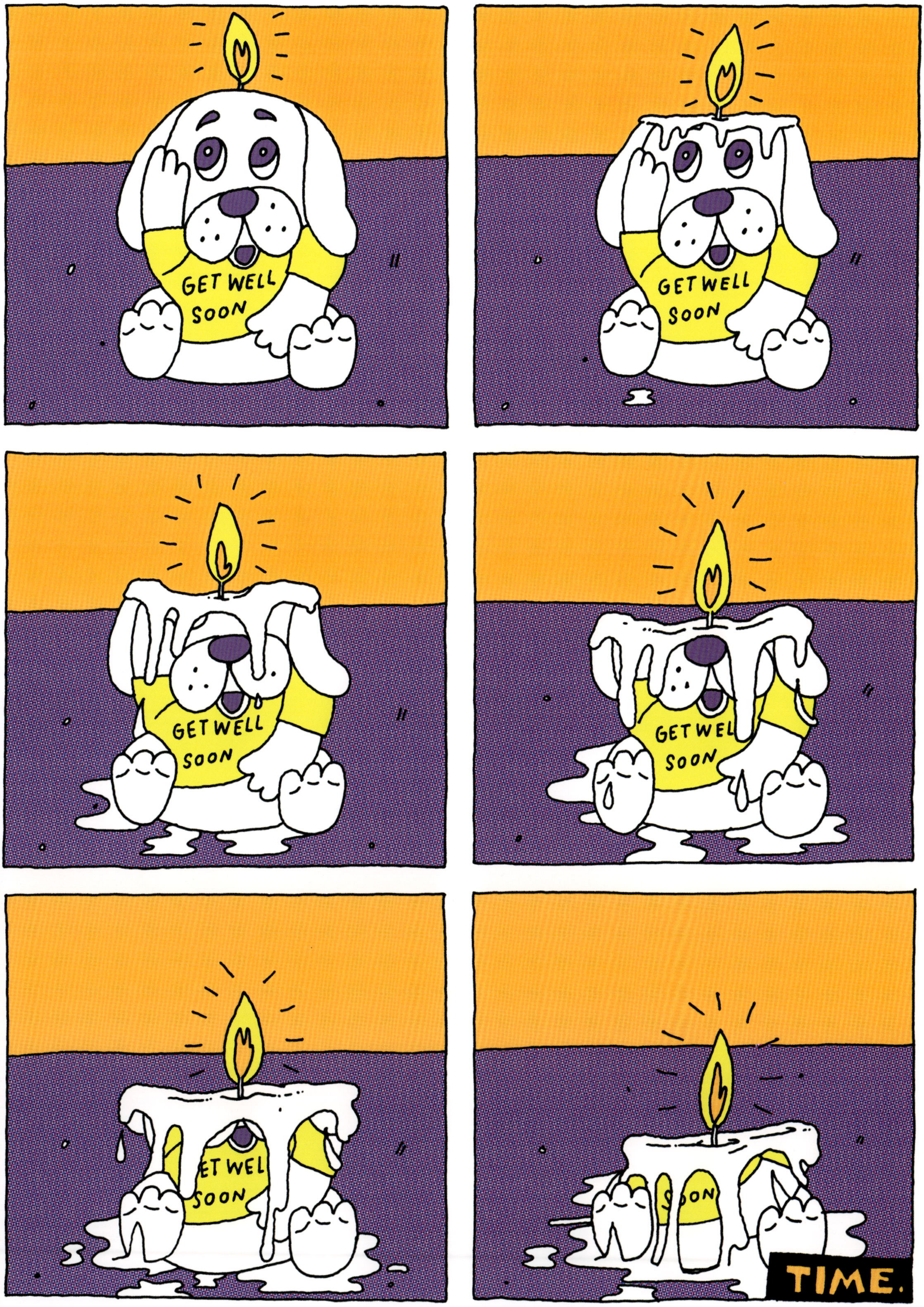
GET WELL SOON
GET WELL SOON
GET WELL SOON
GET WEL SOON
ET WEL SOON
TIME.

Ollie Williams
THOSE DAMN PUNKS ARE SMARTER THAN I THOUGHT!
PURE EVIL!
NUMBING THEIR MINDS WITH SUBSTANCE AND ALCOHOL! FUCK!
GAAHHH! ARGGGGG! CWAHH!
HOW DID THEY KNOW?
BUT LITTLE DO THEY KNOW I HAVE SOMETHING SPECIAL IN STORE FOR THEM! THAT INFOMERCIAL MAY NOT HAVE DONE THE TRICK, BUT THIS WILL!
HA HA HA HA HA HA HA HA HA.
I'M NOT SUPPOSED TO BE CONTAINED! ARGG! LET ME GOOOOO!
HAHAHA THIS TOWN IS DOOMED! ALL THANKS TO THIS PROTOTYPE THOSE ALIENS SOLD TO ME!

AT THAT VERY MOMENT ELSEWHERE...
PIZZA
POOF!
TA DA.
HA HA HA HA HA HA
HA HA HA HA HA
PIZZA
HA HA WATCH THIS!
HEY! PASS THAT BONG MY WAY!
HERE BOSS.
PIZZA
THANKS.
IDIOT.
WHOOSH!
WHAT?
SMASH
HA HA HA HA HA HA HA HA HA HA HA HA
IDIOTS.

GIT DUH MUNNY!
CHA CHING
CHA CHING
CHA CHING
CHA CHING
CO
CHA-CHING!
24 CONVENIENCE
HA... HA... HA.
HA HA.
CHA CHING
CHA CHING
CHA CHING
CHA CHING
CHA CHING
CHA CHING
BANK CO. INT'L
CHA CHING
CHA CHING
CHA CHING
PIECE OF PIZZA
MONEY! HAHA.
CHA, CHING!
C.R.E.A.M.

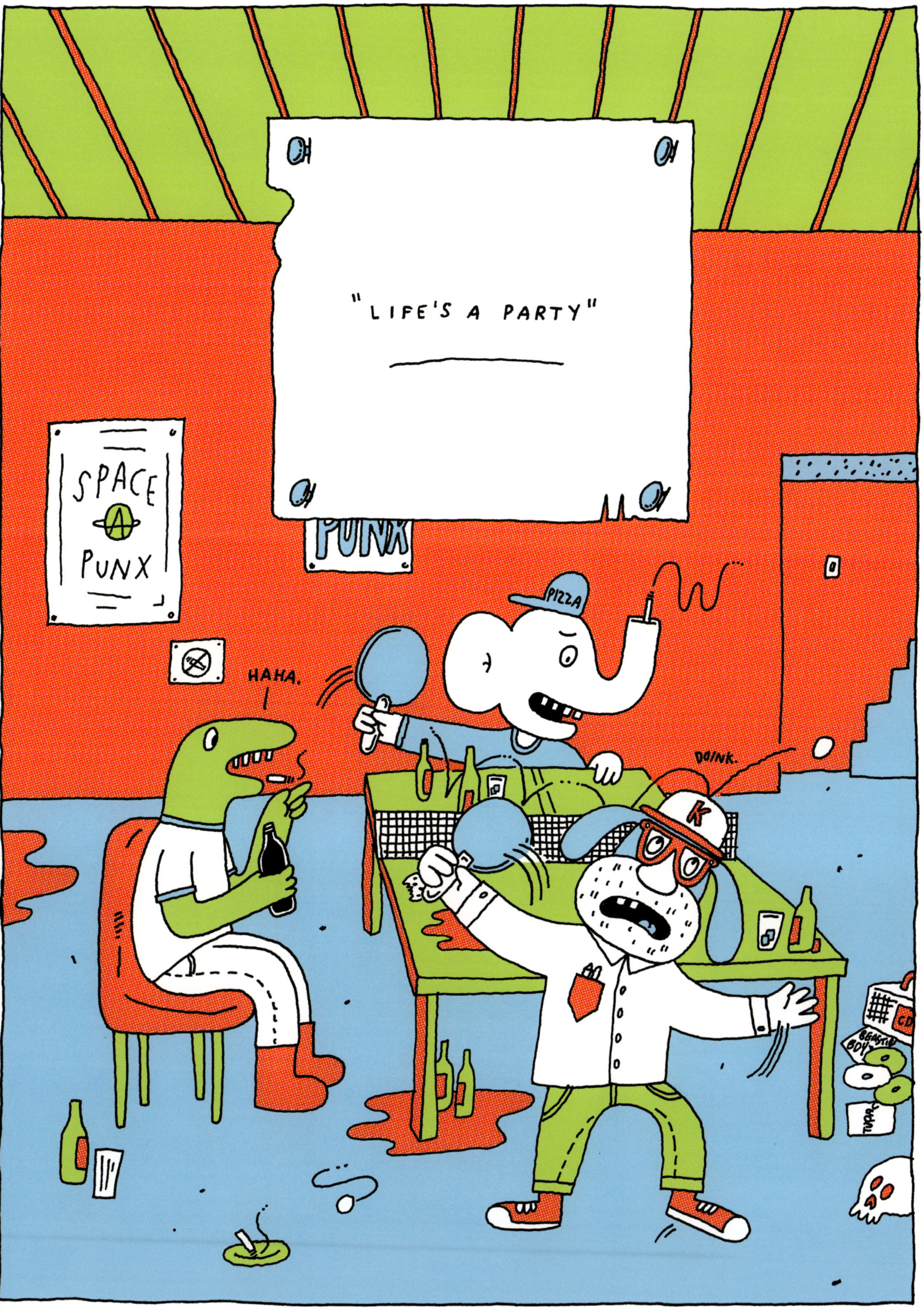

"LIFE'S A PARTY"
SPACE
A
PUNX
PUNX
PIZZA
HAHA.
DOINK.
K

SLURPIE STRIKES BACK
RING RING RING
RING RING RING
SHUT UP!
HELLO...
SLURPIE!
WHAT THE FUCK DO YOU WANT?
SLURPIE! I NEED YOU! I NEED YOU TO DELIVER TONIGHT!
I DON'T KNOW... YOU ARE A HUGE FUCKIN' ASSHOLE.
PLEASE SLURPIE! YOU'RE THE BEST I'VE GOT!
... UNDER ONE CONDITION...
MINUTES LATER:
PIZZA
CLINK.

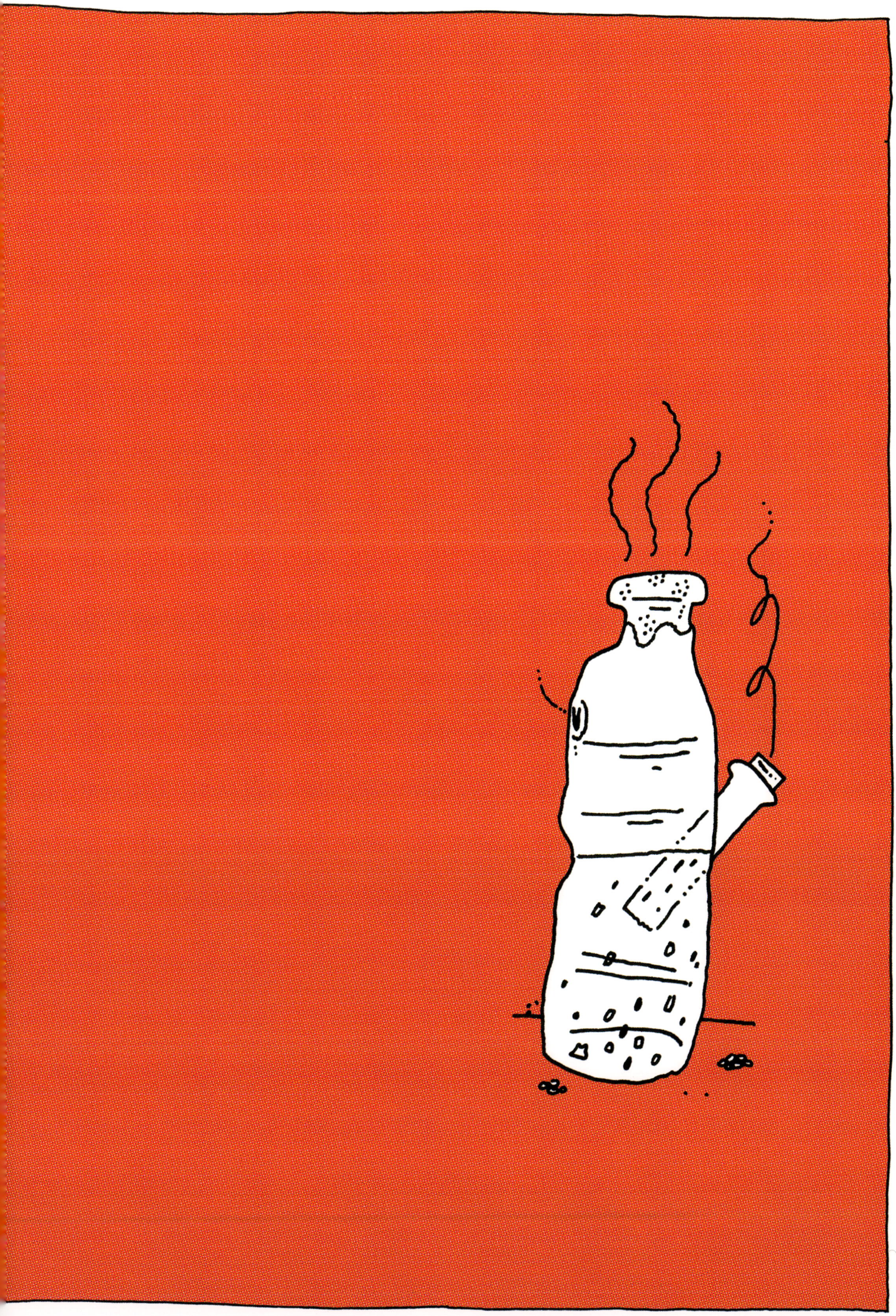

FALL IN LOVE
TICK
TOCK.
COUGH
TICK TOCK
TICK TOCK
SO!
... WHAT'S IT GONNA BE...
?
!
... ARE YOU GONNA KISS ME?
CLICK
TICK.

Panel 1: OUT ON DELIVERY WITH A CAT.

Panel 2: PIZZA / MEOW.

Panel 3: WHAT THE FUCK! / MEOW!

Panel 4: Z P! / WHOA!

Panel 5: HOLY SHIT. / VROOM / MEOW.

Panel 6: OH SHIT! WE'RE BEING FOLLOWED! / AW SHEEEIT!

Panel 7: NOTHIN' LIKE A GOOD OL' FASHIONED U.F.O. CHASE!

Panel 8: 200 KM/HR.

Panel 9: HE'S GAINING ON US! WE'VE GOT TO LOSE SOME WEIGHT. / DEPLOY THE MOUSTACHE GUY!

Panel 10: FDGGSSTTT... / WHAT THE...? / THUMP.

Panel 11: RATS. / ZOOM! / THUNK THUNK / MEOW!

Panel 12: WHAT WAS THAT? / PURR.

"THE COMIC ABOUT THE CATS
THAT LIVE IN THE NEIGHBOURHOOD3"
SSSSSS
!
MEOW?
!
AW FUCK.
R.I.P.

MISSING

Long-haired brown tabby. Answers to 'Kitty'.
Last seen in the Dufferin & Liberty area on September 30. If found, please call:

SLURPIE
▮▮▮3 6▮87

YO MAN I'M IN THE MIDDLE OF NOWHERE!
PIZZA
CAN YOU HEAR ME?
PFF...
I HEAR YA LOUD+CLEAR!
PIZZA.
HELLO!?
HEY!
HEY!
PIZZA
...ARE YOU STILL THERE?
RING
RING
RING
HA HA HA HA HA.
KILL! KILL! KILL!
PHONE

SEALS
SKRIB-
SKRI.
SEALS
SCRATCH-
SCRATCH
?
SEALS
SKRI...
SEALS
SKRIBLE-
SKRABLE-
SKRATCH.
SKRATCH-
SKRIBBLE-
SKRITCH.
FUCK YOU!
FUCK YOU!
SKRIBBLE-
SKRIBLE

FAST FOOD YUM-YUMS
DRIVE THRU
ALRIGHT!!! WHADDA WE GOT HERE?
CHICKEN DOUBLE PATTY ON BUN!
THAT'S ME!
YUM!
NEXT UP... EWWWW VEGI-BURGER, WITH NOTHING ON IT!
GROSS.
REALLY?
UGH SHUT UP!
HA HA
NEXT ON DECK..... ONE DEVILLED EGG!
MMM.
TOSS
AND FINALLY... SOMEONE'S SEVERED.... HAND!...
AHHHHH!
AHHHHH!
AHHHHHH
END.

MONDAY MORNING
CHIRP CHIRP CHIRP CHIRP CHIRP
DID YOU HEAR KERRY DIED?
WHO'S THAT?
THE FUCKING CONVENIENCE STORE GUY DUMBIE!
OHHHH... HIM... SHIT ... HUH.
PIZZA
KHSHT!
I DON'T THINK THIS IS BEER MAN.
HUH?!
WHAT DO YOU MEAN?
I THINK IT'S JUST RUSTY WATER.
WHAT!? ARE YOU SERIOUS?
KRAPPPS
NAH, I'M JOKING.
IT'S KRAPPPS.©
GLUG GLUG GLUG
KRAPPPS
YEEPPP.... DRIVING BEER!

BOOZE HOUNDS
ZOOOM!
200KM/h
URRRRRRK.
SLAM!
ZOOM!
IN THE MIDDLE OF NOWHERE:
THIS SEEMS LIKE A GOOD SPOT!
PHEW!
HA HA.
SURE DOES.
HICK UP.
HA HA.
LET'S SET UP SHOP!
HA.
HICK UP.
FUCK YEAH!
BOOZE
SWING!
TWIST
BEER
GULP
GULP
EASY DOES IT.
SAWW!
PUFF PUFF
SMACK
KEEP OUT
PERRRRFECT.
LET'S STASH THE GOODS OLD CHAP.
CLAP!
STASH.
WINE
CHA CHING
BEER
AW SHIT
RUN!
LET'S GET THE FUCK OUTTA HERE.
KEEP OUT
WHAT FUCKIN' IDIOTS.
HA HA HA ALL MINE!
DUMB FUCKS.
CLINK CLANK.
TEEFED.

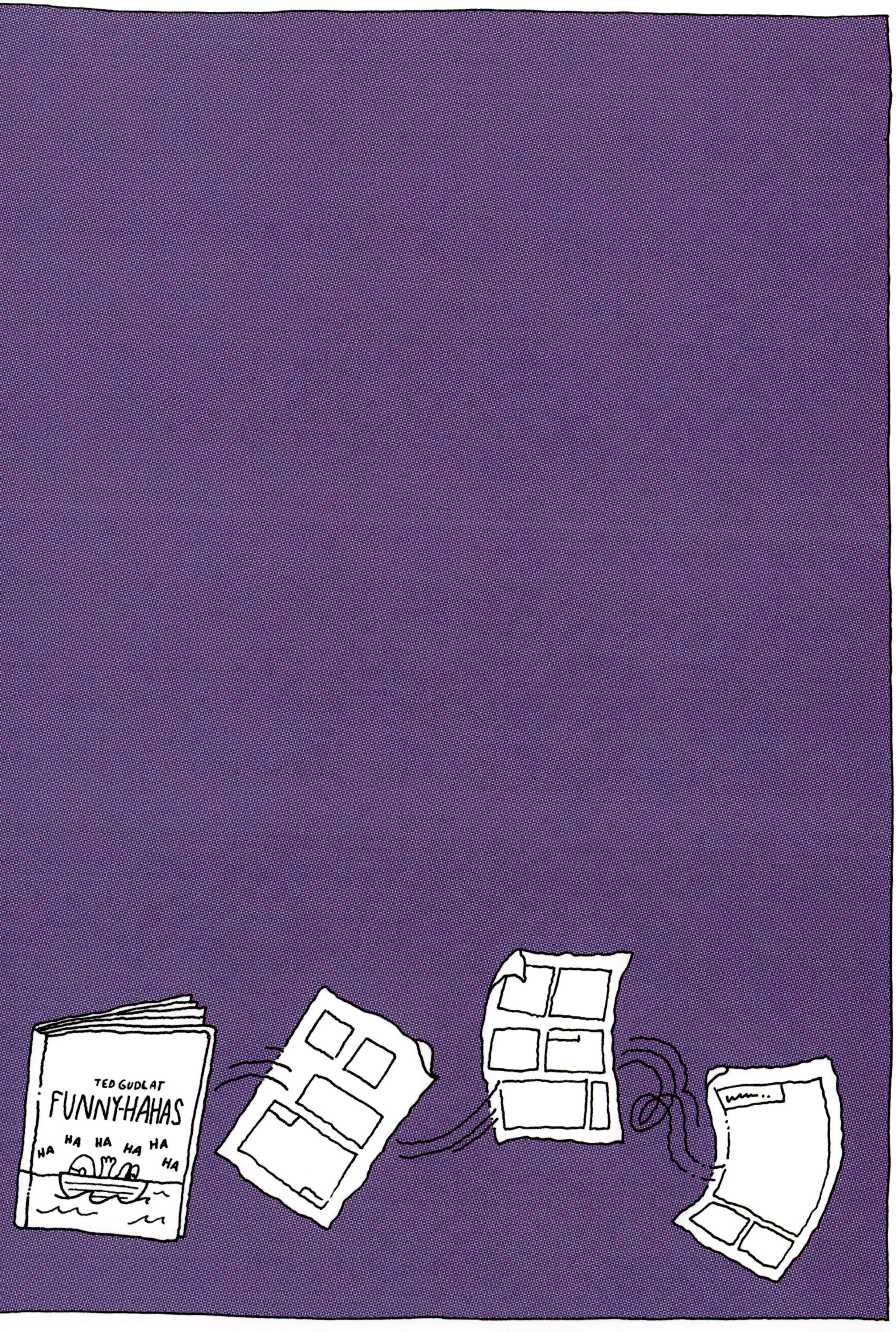
TED GUDLAT
FUNNY-HAHAS
HA HA HA HA HA HA

At the Bottom of the Lake:

HELP! ME!

"THIS GUY IS DOOOOMED."

"NO KIDDING."

"SEND HELP PLEASE!"

"THINK WE SHOULD AT LEAST TRY TO HELP?"

"..... NAAA."

"WANT TO GO MAKE BABIES?"

"ABSOLUTELY."

"WHAT?"

"NOOO WAIT! COMEBACK! WHY?"

A PORTAL IN TIME.
WHY HELLO AND WELCOME TO THE FUTURE.
DO YOU REALLY THINK IT'S THAT AWFUL? ARE YOU WONDERING HOW I AM STILL TALKING TO YOU?
IT'S THE FUTURE!
THE FUTURE ISN'T A PLACE OR A TIME. IT IS SIMPLY A STATE OF MIND.
STAY POSITIVE AND IT MIGHT BE OKAY!
DIDN'T THINK IT WOULD END UP THIS WAY DID YOU? WHAT IS EVEN HAPPENING?
DROP BY DROP, SIP BY SIP. PIZZA LUNCH YUM YUM!
DO YOU DESIRE ANYTHING? I CAN GRANT YOU TWO WISHES! YOU KNOW I CAN DO THAT RIGHT?
NAH! I WAS JUST SHITTIN' YOU. THE FUTURE ISN'T THAT COOL! ....
YOU SHOULD REWARD YOURSELF WITH AN ICE COLD BEER!
AFTER ALL YOU HAVE TRAVELLED A LONG WAY.
THE FUTURE HOLDS ALL THE ANSWERS. BUT YOU MIGHT AS WELL JUST WAIT FOR TOMORROW.
BECAUSE THE TRUTH SOMETIMES CAN HURT YOU.
...AND MAKE YOU WISH YOU WERE NEVER BORN!
DOG IS MAN'S BEST FRIEND.
THINK FAST IT'S THE FUTURE! BUT THINK SLOW BECAUSE SOMEONE IS PROBABLY READ-ING YOUR MIND!
DON'T LIE TO YOURSELF, LIE TO SOMEONE ELSE IT'S THE FUTURE. DOG EAT DOG... SURVIVAL OF THE FITTEST.
HOLD YOUR BREATH + COUNT TO TEN.
IF YOU HOLD YOUR BREATH YOU WON'T LIVE FOREVER. YOU'LL PROBABLY MISS A LOT OF STUFF!
HEY! AND GOOD FRIENDS ARE HARD TO FIND SO BE THANK-FUL FOR THE ONE'S YOU HAVE GOT!
WELL, IT WAS NICE MEETING YOU! MAYBE ONE DAY WE WILL MEET AGAIN. FAREWELL!
POOF!
...AND HE'S GONE.

FAMILY RESTAURANT
YUMMM BURGERS!
HEARD THEY HAVE NEW MANAGEMENT.
MIGHT BE A GOOD TIME!
HEY GUYS. WELCOME TO FAMILY RESTAURANT FEEL FREE TO SIT ANYWHERE YOU LIKE.
WHAT YOU STARIN' AT?
HMM.
YEAH.
OUTSIDERS?
WHY ARE THEY HERE?
PIZZA
HMMMM
GRRRRR.
SOMETHING SEEMS A LITTLE DIFFERENT ABOUT THIS PLACE.
PIZZA
AGREED!
NOT A BAD SPOT!
I BET THE FOOD WILL BE DELICIOUS.
IT'S NEW AND IMPROVED!
PIZZA
TWO ORDERS OF THE CHEF'S SPECIAL.
PIZZA
ALIVE!
IT'S!
AAAAH...
PIZZA
GROSS.
HISSSS
BLINK
wiggle
YOU BETTER EAT UP, OR I'LL KICK YER ASS!

HAVE YOU NOTICED ANYTHING KIND OF FUNNY ABOUT THE PEOPLE IN TOWN THE PAST COUPLE WEEKS?
NO WHY?
PIZZA
I DON'T KNOW I JUST FEEL LIKE SHIT HAS GOTTEN A LITTLE FUCKED UP THAT'S ALL.
I'M NOT FOLLOWING- SORRY MAN.
PIZZA
WELL I DON'T KNOW... I JUST FEEL LIKE ALL THE FAMILIAR FACES IN TOWN ARE BEING WASHED OUT BY A BUNCH OF SKETCHY IDIOTS.
NOPE, HAVEN'T NOTICED.
PIZZA
YOU'RE TELLING ME YOU DON'T THINK ANYTHING STRANGE IS GOING ON? NOTHING... ZIP... ZILCHE ... ZERO?
THAT IS WHAT I AM TELLING YOU.
PIZZA
SO YOU'RE SAYING NOTHING WEIRD OR REMOTELY ODD HAS HAPPENED TO YOU IN THE PAST FEW DAYS?
THAT'S WHAT I'M SAYING.
PIZZA
SIGH
I HOPE HE'S BUYING THIS.
PIZZA

WHOOPSIES
YAH, LAMAR IS A FUCKIN' TRAIN WRECK. I LET HIM BORROW MY CAR TODAY TO FIGURE HIS LIFE OUT.
PIZZA
YEAH, HE HAS REALLY BEEN BLOWIN' IT.
I TRY TO HAVE PATIENCE FOR THE GUY BUT IT'S HARD SOMETIMES.
PIZZA
UH-OH.
CRASH.
COFFEE
USE THIS
RECYCLE
HISSSS.
PIZZA
A WRITE OFF

WALDORF TOWER APARTMENTS
WHERE'S LAMAR WITH THE SHIT!
FRIG
HE'LL BE OUT SOON. JUST HOLD YOUR HORSES.
120 BONES BABY MAN.
FUCK YEAH!
MEOW LYFE
GRUNT GRUNT GRUNT
UHG.
DEAR GOD, THANK YOU FOR THIS DELICIOUS FOOD + PLEASE KILL THE ALIENS BEFORE THEY KILL US.
!
HELP! INTRUDERS!
KICK!
HELP!
CRY.

A TALE OF COLD PIES
STARRING: SLURPIE
SLURPIE! I NEED YOU TO WORK TONIGHT.
PIZZA
I CAN'T. LAMAR CRASHED MY CAR.
GOD DAMMIT SLURPIE, YOU'RE THE WORST EMPLOYEE THAT HAS EVER WORKED HERE!
ALRIGHT, ALRIGHT. I'LL FIGURE SOMETHING OUT! I THINK I'VE GOT AN IDEA.
PIZZA
SLAM!
WOW.
PIZZA'S HERE!
OH MY!
PIZZA
PIZZA
PIZZA
WAIT A SECOND! THIS PIZZA IS FREEZING COLD!
ZIP
PIZZA
PIZZA
PIZZA
AND SOAKING WET!!!
THANKS FOR ORDERING PIECE-OF-PIZZA!©
HEY GET BACK HERE!
DUM DUM DUM DUM DUM DUM DUM DUM
RING RING

HA HA HA HA
HA HA HA.
HA HA HA
HA HA HA.
HA HA
HA HA HA
HA HA!
HUH?!
WELCOME
STRANGER.
WOULD YOU LIKE AN
ALCOHOLIC BEVERAGE?
WE HAVEN'T SEEN
ANYBODY FOR WEEKS.
YES, WE'VE BEEN
WAITING FOR A
MAN LIKE YOU!
WOOOOOO!
WE LOVE YOU.
FOUND.

"THE COMIC ABOUT THE CATS IN THE NEIGHBOURHOOD 4"
ZZZ
MEOW REOW?
ZZZZZ
!
WHACK!
SMACK!
CRACK!
SWOOSH!
GASP...
MEOW...
$1
I'M SORRY...

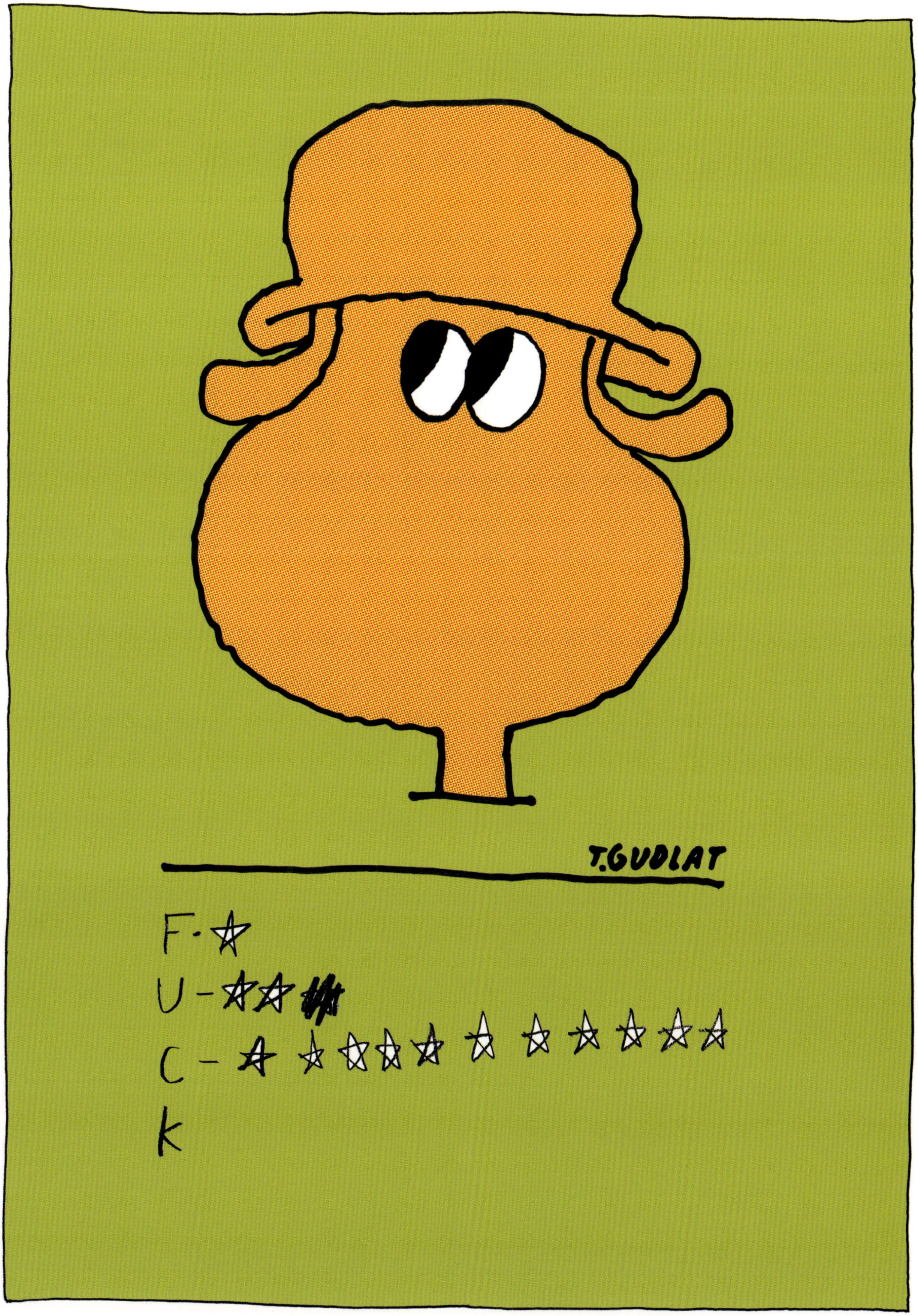
T.GUDLAT
F·
U-
C-
K

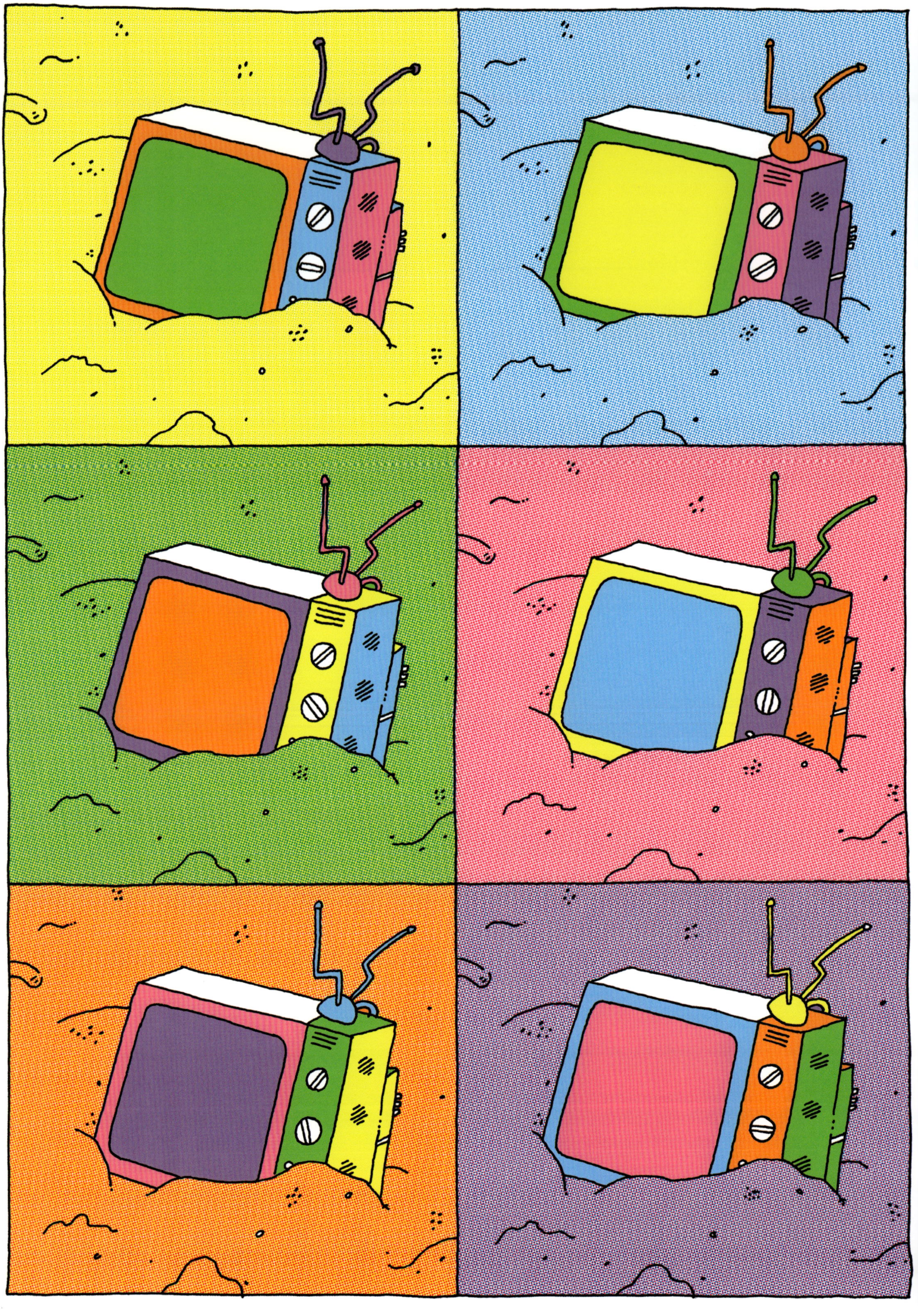

AT THE CAT'S HOUSE:
WOAH
THIS IS A PAID ADVERTISEMENT BROUGHT TO YOU BY INFOCORP.
DO YOU HAVE HOLES IN YOUR POCKETS?
YOU
NO MONEY.
NOOO MONEY.
NO! MONEY!
I MUST!
CH
VOL
WHY ARE YOU JUST SITTING ON THE COUCH EATING POTATO CHIPS?
MUNCH...
LIFE COULD BE...
...EASY!
YAHOO!
SPEED BOAT
YOU'RE IN TOTAL CONTROL!
GET UP AND DO SOMETHING.
HOORAY!
PHONE BOOTH
WINK
CALL NOW!
CH
VOL
WE KNOW YOU'RE A BUSY PERSON!
BLAH BLAH BLAH
SOOOOOOOOOOO... ...IF YOU CALL NOW WE WILL MAKE THE FIRST PAYMENT FOR YOU!!!
IT TAKES...
TICK
TOCK
TICK
SECONDS!
DON'T MISS OUT ON THIS LIMITED TIME TELEVISION OFFER!
HELP!
EARLY·BIRD·SPECIAL!
OLD LIFE
CALL NOW!
NEW LIFE!
YOUR NEW LIFE AWAITS YOU!
REACH PERFECTION.
BUT WAIT THERE IS...
CH
VOL
MORE!
LIFE GOES ON.

SPACEPUNX
?
SSSSSSSSSS...
WHY ME?
RAIL ROAD
HAHA HA.
BIKE
HEY LOOK GUYS. I FOUND A QUARTZ!
NO TRESPASSIN'

SPACE PUNX
VENUE
TONIGHT ONLY: AZTEC TEENZ / CONTACT HIGH
COVER! 10 BUX!
BLAH BLAH BLAH BABY BABY MAN!
OH MY GOD! LOOK WHO IT IS! LIZZIE!
CONTACT
AZTEC TEENZ
WHY WOULD SHE SHOW HER FUCKING FACE HERE?
BEATS ME, MAYBE SHE LIKES CONTACT HIGH?
SHUT UP. I'M GONNA KICK HER ASS IF SHE EVEN COMES CLOSE TO ME.
OK!
YAA YAA! LALA CACA!
WHAT THE FUCK! SHE'S LOOKING RIGHT AT US. LOOK AWAY PRETEND WE DON'T SEE HER.
UGH!
THAT FUCKING BITCH KNOWS EXACTLY HOW TO FUCK WITH ME!
THANK YOU! THANK YOU!

NEWS@SIX
... AND THAT'S WHY EXPERTS SAY THERE IS SO MUCH BLOOD IN THE DRINKING WATER.
LOCAL EYE
MOB DRAINS BODY
NEWS @6
WAIT A SECOND. I'M GETTING A LIVE FEED IN MY EARPIECE!
LIVE FEED...
NEWS @6
I AM BEING INFORMED THAT... GIANT... ALIENS... HAVE... INVADED OUR DOWNTOWN!
LIVE
LEAVE NOW!!!
NEWS @6
IT IS SUGGESTED THAT EVERYBODY LEAVE TOWN IMMEDIATELY!
GIANT CREATURES!
NEWS @6
I REPEAT LEAVE TOWN! GET THE HELL OUT!!
I KNOW I AM!
NEWS @6
MAN WHAT ELSE IS ON?
SWITCH!
YA THAT SUCKED. THIS IS MUCH BETTER.
YA I LIKE THIS ONE.
HEY STOP HOGGIN' THAT JOINT!
OH YEAH. HERE MAN.
PIZZA
FFP FFP FPP.
SPACEPUNX
HA HA HA HA HA HA
HA HA HA HA HA.
SMASH.

KERRY LIVES

"WHA... WHAT?"

"WHERE AM I?"

"WHAT TIME IS IT?"

"WAIT A SECOND... NO MORE ROPES! NO MORE CRIMINALS!"

"EXCEPT I'M IN THIS CAVE."

"HMM."

"AH HA!"

"I GUESS THERE IS LIGHT AT THE END OF THE TUNNEL."

LEEP!

SHUFFLE

....

!

...

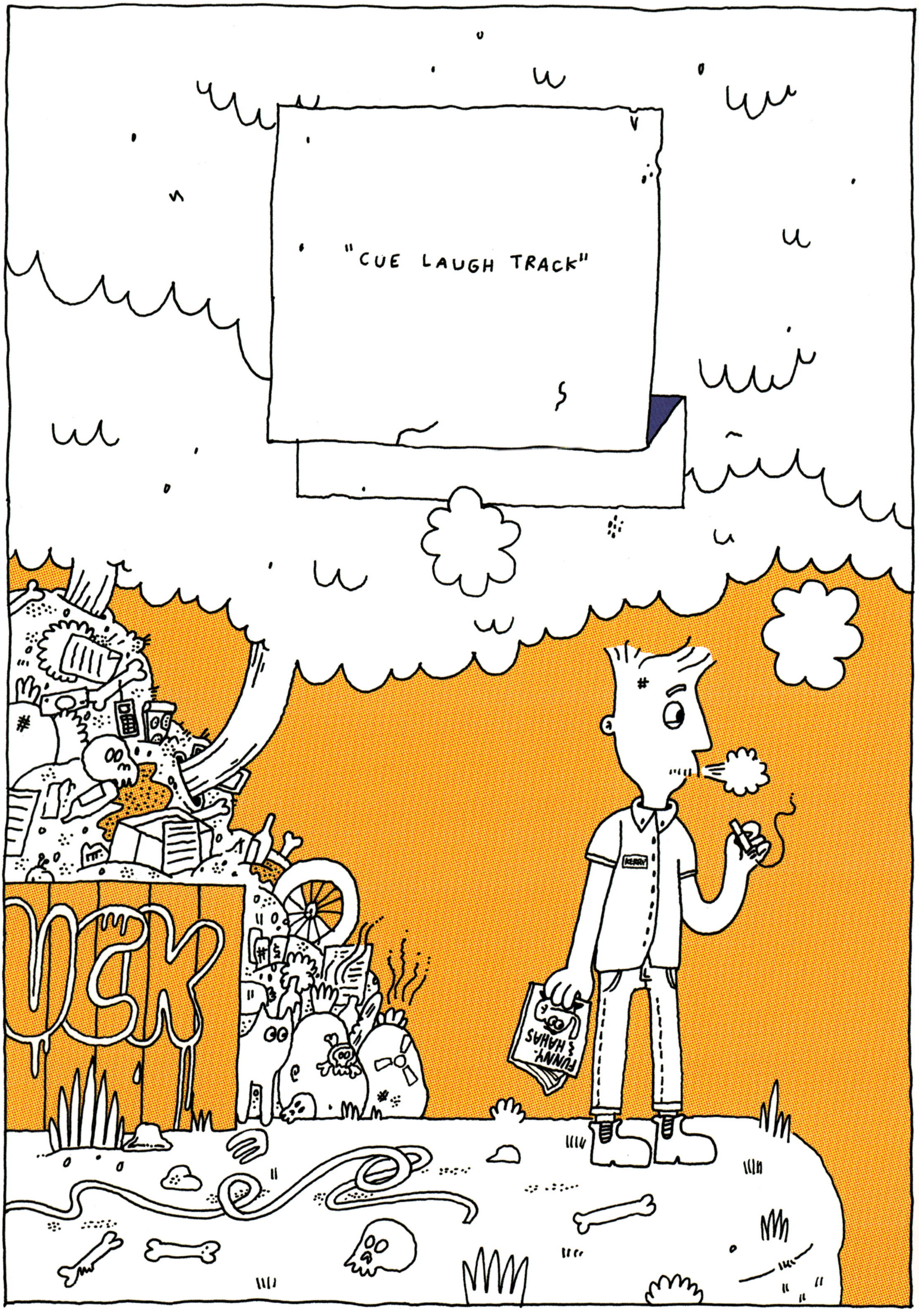
"CUE LAUGH TRACK"

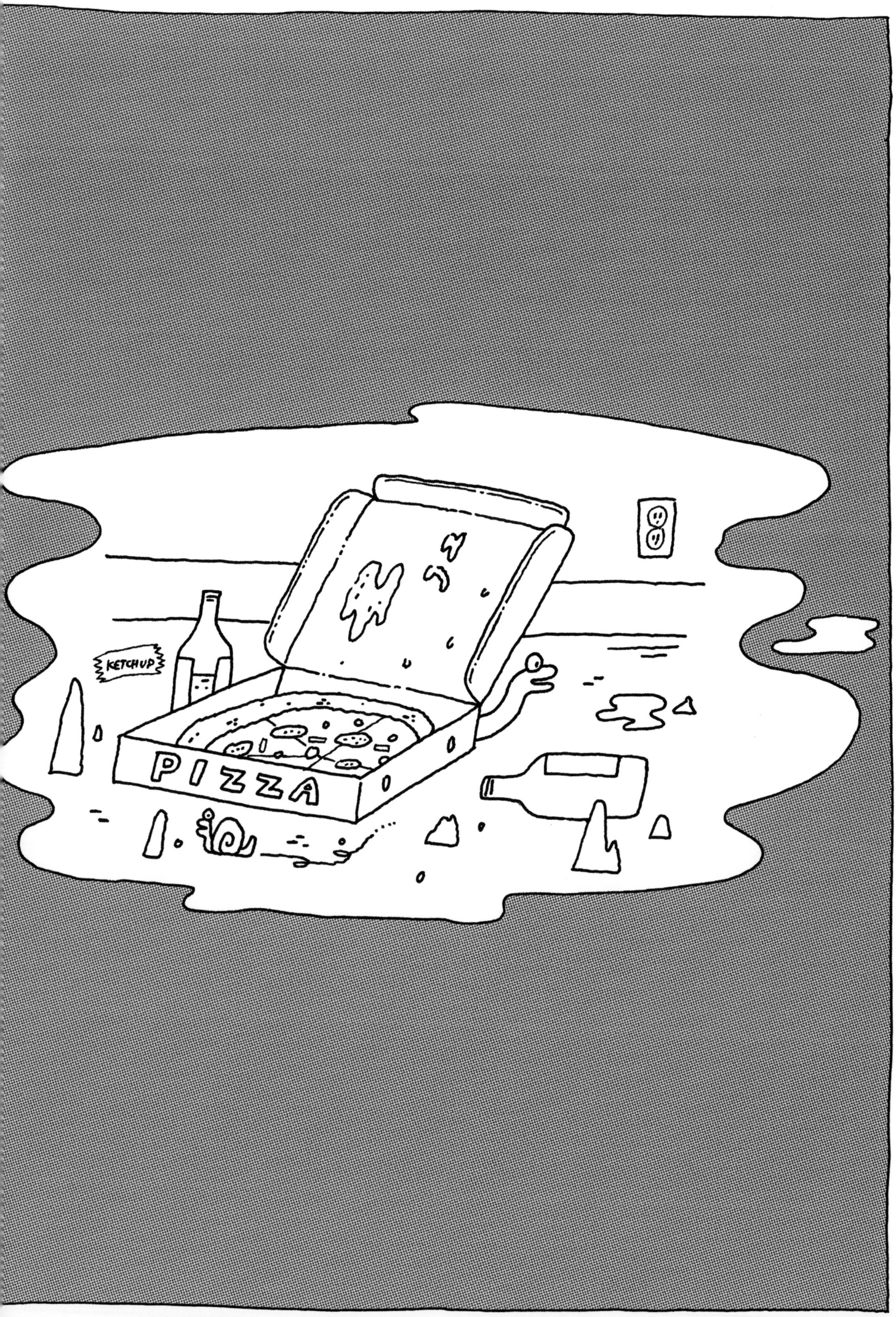
KETCHUP
PIZZA

INFOCRAP.
INFO CRAP 2
TOYS
IWAAAA
McDO
DRINK
CARTOONS
FAST INSURA
PETS
INTERNET
NTS CO.
SMASH
HA HA HA
DIAMONDS
VESTME
BANK
HOTEL
BREAD
SMACK
SNAP!
SEX
FART.
STOP
MONOPOLY
SCREECH
FREE HAIR
HISSS
POOF!
BEERS
CIGARETTES
SCHOOL
BEER
SHOESTORE
PIZZA

FUN FACTS:
STUFF YOU MAY OR MAY NOT HAVE PICKED UP ON. YOU PROBABLY DON'T CARE ANYWAY.
SLURPIE IS AN ELEPHANT.
YO!
HE LIVES/LIVED IN A TREEFORT AND DELIVERS PIZZA
SLURPIE'S SEDAN:
PIZZA
THE CAR LOOKS DIFFERENT IN EVERY STRIP. HE BOUGHT IT FOR 400$ ON CRAIGSLIST.
LAMAR IS A CROCODILE HE'S A BIG IDIOT SOMETIMES.
HE CRASHES SLURPIE'S CAR, BURNS HIS HOUSE DOWN AND BLAH BLAH BLAH.
SLURPIE'S TREEFORT PRIOR TO BURNING.
PRETTY SWEET.
ALIENS WANT MONEY.
MONEY
NOW!
BUY!
A SERIES OF EVIL INFO-MERCIALS ARE MEANT TO BRAINWASH THE TOWN.
E-DOGG: WOKE UP FEELIN' SHITTY AGAIN THIS MORNING.
HE IS A DOG BUT NOT LIKE A DOG DOG...
CONVENIENCE STORE GETS ROBBED.
200.00
KERRY GETS POPPED.
THIS IS SLURPIE'S BOSS
PIZZA
HE HAS MOOD SWINGS A LOT AND TREATS PEOPLE POORLY.
INFOCORP TOWERS ARE ERECTED. TOWERS OVER ALL OTHER BUILDINGS.
INFOCORP
INFO CORP 2
OILLIE WILLIAMS IS THE VILLIAN. HE'S NOT SMART AND HE'S CRAZY. HE TRADES HIS MONEY TO THE ALIENS.
HAHA
MARV GETS LOST AT SEA:
HAHAHA
... HE FUCKIN' LOVES IT.
EVERYONE GETS THEIR PIZZA FROM HERE.
YUM.
PIECE-OF-PIZZA©.
THERE ARE 3 TYPES OF ALIENS:
KISS ME!
KILL.
ALIEN-ALIENS
DOG ALIENS
RAT ALIENS.
LET'S SHAKE HANDS.
DON'T WORRY.
KERRY Z. IS NOT DEAD OR ALIVE. SUPER META.
HE IS THE LAST SOUL TO WALK THE EARTH.
WHENEVER I CLOSED MY EYES THERE WERE SNAKES EVERYWHERE!
NOW THANKS TO BLOOD OF JESUS OIL THE SNAKES ARE ALL GONE.
Z Z Z
THIS GUY!
SLURPIE GETS FIRED, AND THEN REHIRED.
THEN IS FORCED TO BIKE TO DELIVER PIZZAS
YUK, YUK. I'M NOT EVEN IN THIS BOOK!
PSST. SLURPIE'S AN ALCOHOLIC AND THE NUTMEG WASN'T REAL.
NICK'S PIZZA BAR IS THE BEST PLACE FOR BEER.
NICK'S PIZZA BAR
THEY CLOSED DOWN THOUGH.
ENROD.
HE'S A TOTAL LIABILITY.
NOTHING BECOMES OF THE BAND. THEY SUCK.
K
KJ AND THE JUICERS RULE!
THE TOWN IS AN OLD MINING TOWN. THAT'S ALL YOU FIND OUT.
KITTY. RAW. REAL.
A DIRECT COMMENT ON SOCIETY
KITTY.
EVERYONE DIED.
POOF!
NOW WE'RE ALL A LITTLE DUMBER.

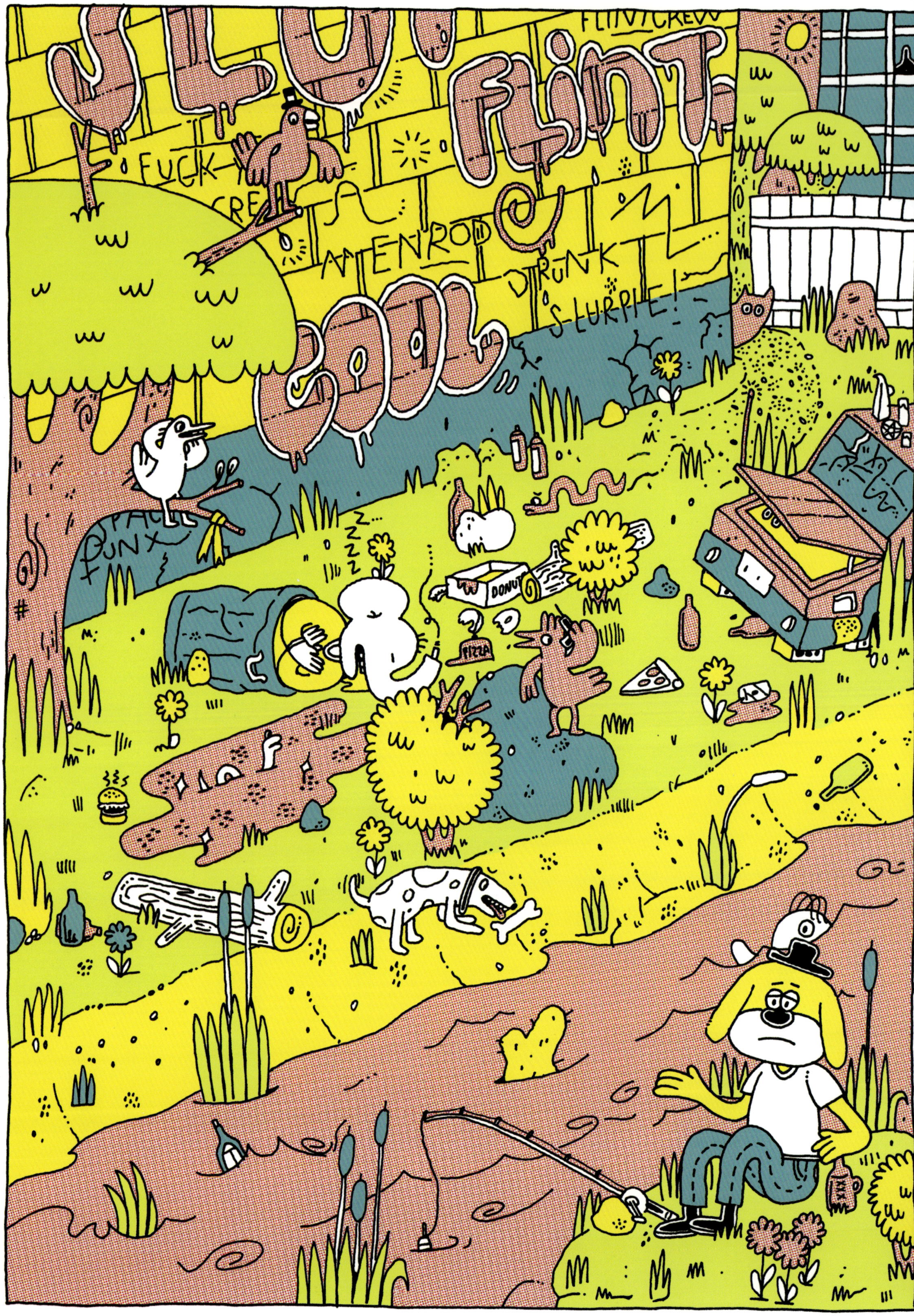
FLINT
DRUNK
SLURPIE!
DONUT
PIZZA

SHINY EYEBALLS
GUITAR SOLO PLAYS THROUGHOUT ENTIRE COMIC.
CLICK CLICK CLICK
THERE IS SOMETHING ABOUT THIS GAME THAT JUST DOESN'T SEEM RIGHT...
CLICK CLICK
CLICK CLICK
...BUT I CAN'T QUITE PUT MY FINGER ON IT.
CLICK CLICK
BEEP.
BUTTON
BUTTON
WORLD DESTROYER
WHAT ON EARTH ARE YOU EVEN TALKING ABOUT?
CLICK
CLICK
I FORGOT.
WWOOOWWWW!
OH NOOO!
WHERE EARTH WAS.
CLICK CLICK
CLICK
CLICK
CONGRATULATIONS!
NEW ALIEN PLANET.
THEN THE ALIENS HAD A PARTY AND NO HUMANS EVER EXISTED AGAIN!

SPACE PUNX!
MISSING: RESPONDS TO KITTY. CALL SLURPIE.
"SLURPIE"
CAT PLAN-
SH
2015

"THROW BACK CLASSICS" — "HIGHLY COLLECTABLE!" RE-ISSUED FOR YOUR ENJOYMENT!	SLURPIE	E-DOGG
"WHO GIVES A SHIT?" LAMAR	KEITH	"HA HA HA HA HA HA HA HA!" MARV
KERRY Z.	ENROD	"BROOOW?" KITTY

E-DOGG
BLOODHOUND

WEARS A SCARF EVEN WHEN IT'S NOT COLD.

QUOTES: "WHERE'S THE TOBACCO?" "YOU GOT TOBACCO?"

WALKS REAL DOGS.

IS AS BROKE AS I AM.

SLURPIE
ELEPHANT

DELIVERS PIZZAS FOR "PIECE OF PIZZA".

LIKES TO HAVE A GOOD TIME, FRIENDS ALWAYS COME FIRST.

HAS HIS VICES

LIVES IN THE COOLEST TREE HOUSE EVER.

ARTIFACT

MARV
QUESTIONABLE

WILL DO PRETTY MUCH ANYTHING YOU ASK HIM TO DO.

IS A CHILDREN'S BOOK AUTHOR/ILLUSTRATOR.

LIKES RUM AND COKES.

ROLLS THE BEST "L" PAPE.

KEITH
MUPPET

"THE GODFATHER"

IF YOU HAVE A PROBLEM IT HAS ALREADY HAPPENED TO KEITH AND HE'LL TELL YOU NOT TO WORRY.

MAKES AN INSANE SANDWICH.

QUOTE: "LET'S GO EAT SOME GARBAGE."

LAMAR
CROCODILE

FUCKING ANCIENT.

LOVES A GOOD BARGAIN.

WILL NEVER LET YOU HEAR THE END OF IT.

ALSO WILL NEVER DIE BECAUSE OF A DEAL HE MADE WITH ANCIENT MAGICAL GODS.

KITTY
FELINE

NEVER TAKES NO FOR AN ANSWER.

KNOWS PEOPLE WHO'LL KILL YOU, IF HE DOESN'T.

WOULD EAT YOU IF YOU WERE SMALLER THAN HIM.

AKA: FAKE SNOOPY

ENROD
SHITTY PHARAOH

A GOOD FRIEND BUT CAN BE ANNOYING.

13 YEARS OLD BUT HAS BEEN ALIVE FOR AGES.

ALWAYS DOWN TO CHILL

QUOTE: "TWIST UP A BUD!"

SHIT HEAD STATUS.

KERRY 2.
GOOD GUY

WORKS/WORKED AT THE 24 HOUR CONVENIENCE.

HAS BEEN MISSING FOR WEEKS.

HAS DIED A FEW TIMES.

THERE IS A LITTLE KERRY 2. IN ALL OF US. LIKE A "BABY" KERRY.

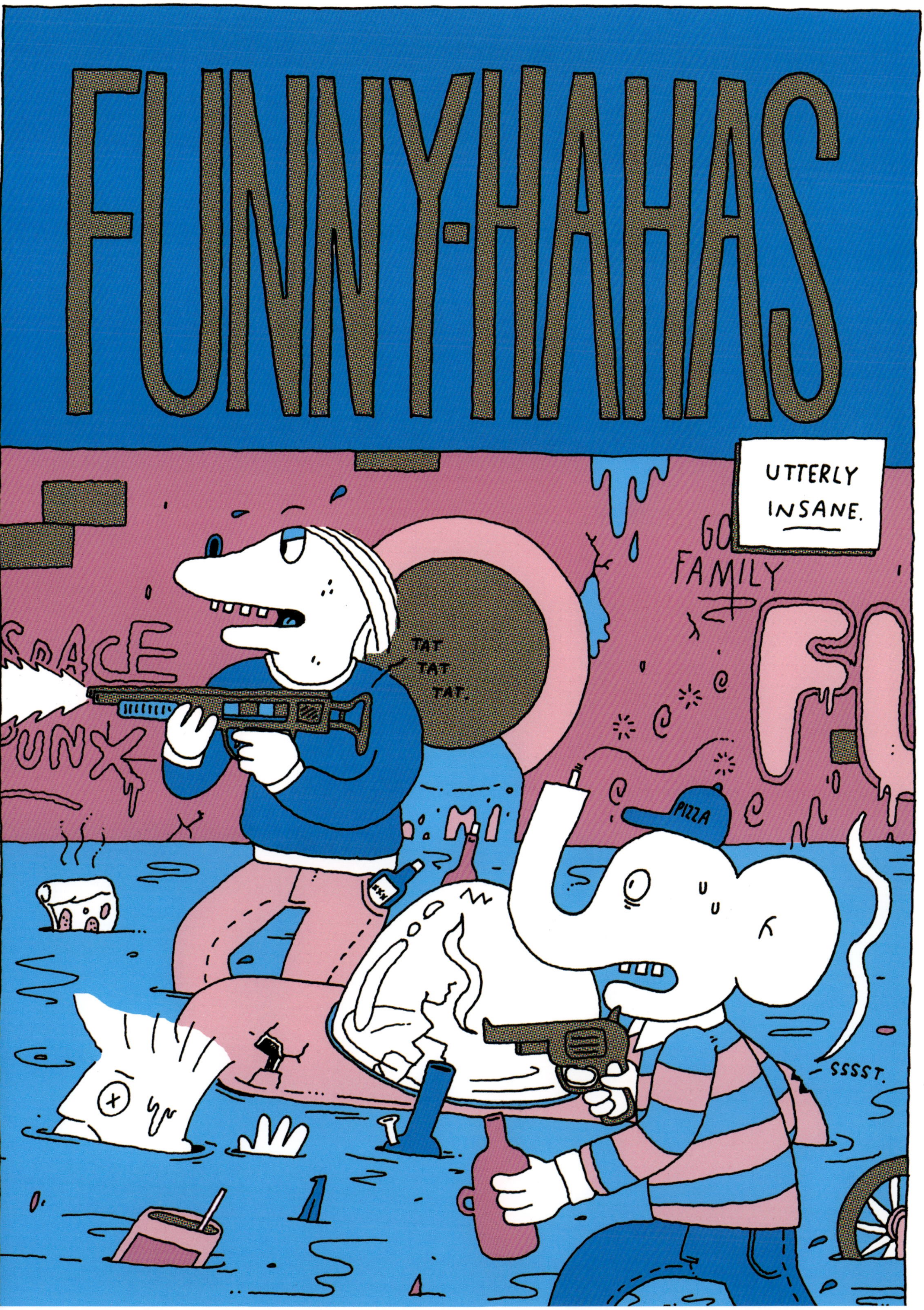
FUNNY-HAHAS
UTTERLY INSANE.
GO FAMILY
SPACE PUNX
TAT TAT TAT.
PIZZA
SSSST.

Ted Gudlat is a cartoonist from Toronto, Ontario. He has self-published several hand-printed collections of his comics and this is his first full-length book with ROADS Publishing. His comics are created using traditional materials and are coloured digitally. He dreams of one day living in a tree fort and delivering pizzas, just like Slurpie.

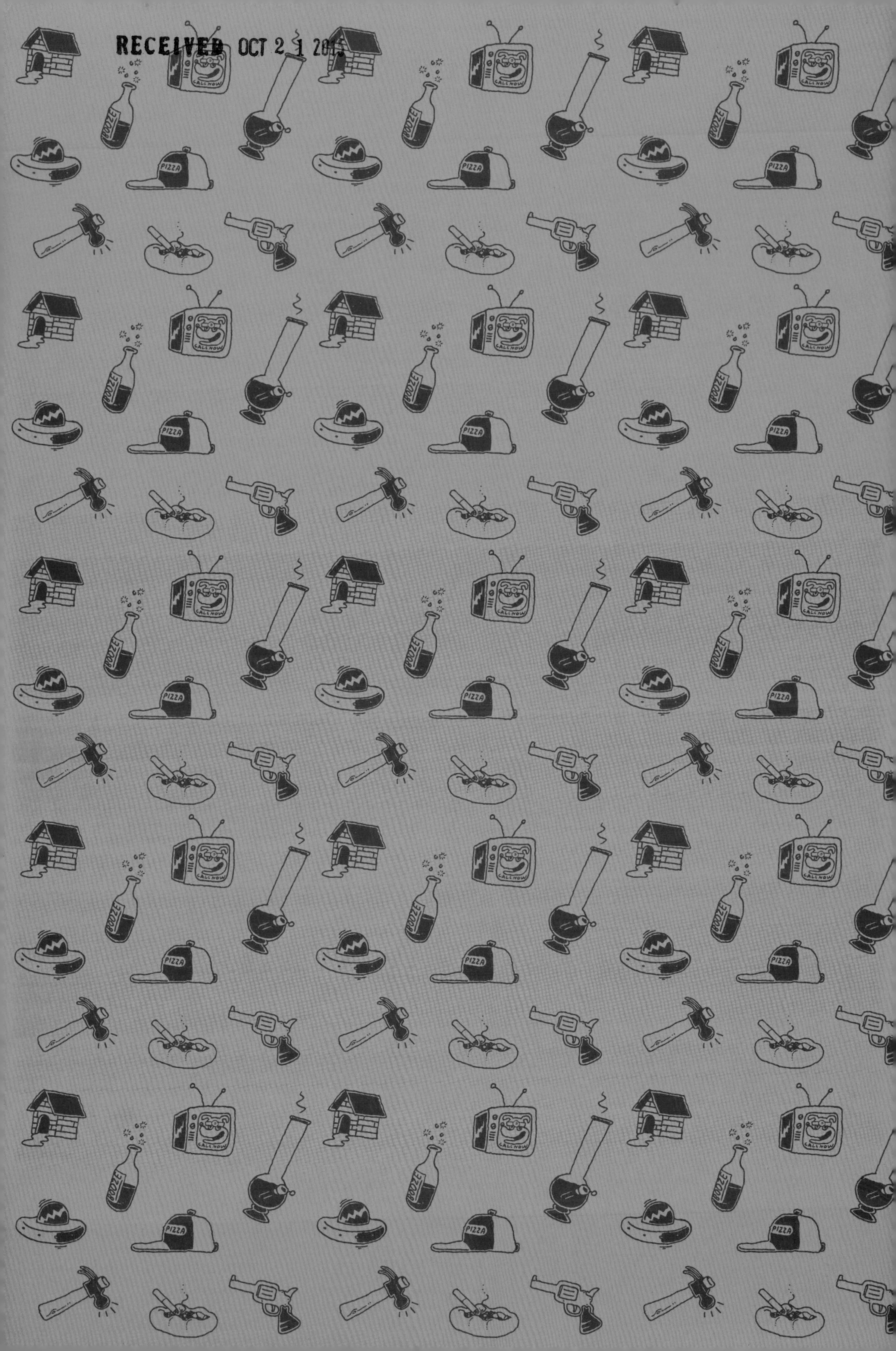
BOOZE!
PIZZA
CALL NOW